AF342378

TWO LIVES HAD I—
ONE WAS A DRAG!!

TWO LIVES HAD I— ONE WAS A DRAG!!

An Autobiography

TOM DEVLIN

VANTAGE PRESS
New York

FIRST EDITION

All rights reserved, including the right of
reproduction in whole or in part in any form.

Copyright © 1996 by Tom Devlin

Published by Vantage Press, Inc.
516 West 34th Street, New York, New York 10001

Manufactured in the United States of America
ISBN: 0-533-11705-4

Library of Congress Catalog Card No.: 95-90778

0 9 8 7 6 5 4 3 2 1

To all my beautiful friends, living and dead without whose help
past and present this book could not have been written

TWO LIVES HAD I—
ONE WAS A DRAG!!

ONE

As far back as I can recall, my life had been on the quiet side, with nothing out of the ordinary happening. Even the usual childhood illnesses were spared me, although I naturally came in contact with children who had chicken pox, measles, whooping cough, and so forth. I also slept with my young brother during the time he had chicken pox and still didn't contract it. At times I thought that perhaps there was something wrong with me because I didn't contract these diseases. How thankful I am now that I was so fortunate.

I suppose my childhood was about as normal as any other child's with the exception that I didn't care much for the usual games that most boys played. Baseball was the farthest thing from my mind, as were fishing and hunting. However, I did enjoy hiking in the warm weather and couldn't wait until the first warm Saturday in the spring, when some friends and I would take off for a hiking trip to New Jersey. That was a really big deal for us in those days. But now, the mere mention of walking to the corner store sends shivers through me. As long as there is public transportation and taxicabs, walking is something I rarely do; unless, of course, it's absolutely necessary.

I didn't bother with girls too much or, I should say, as much as other boys in the neighborhood. I enjoyed playing with girls (and some of their games as well), even to the extent of dressing like them on Thanksgiving, when we would go "begging." I used to look forward to it each year with great anticipation. No doubt this was to lay the groundwork for my future, although at the time I had no possible way of knowing it or to what extent it would change my way of life. Looking back with amusement now, I somehow can't believe I was so naive and innocent about so many things. I will try to describe some of the things that happened to me.

By way of introduction, my name is Tom Devlin. My parents were Irish-English, Roman Catholic; I have a younger brother and two younger sisters. I have blonde hair, blue eyes, stand five feet six inches tall, and weigh 122 pounds.

In 1949, at the age of nineteen, I was working for a large motion picture company. I had few friends and kept pretty much to myself. I never considered myself attractive, although the girls in school said I was "cute." I might have had a perfect V shape, had it not been for my large rib cage. I never gave much thought to my appearance and wore clothes that seemed too large for me.

I had been corresponding for a few years with a friend from high-school days who was now living in Chicago. I knew that Harold Trou was quite effeminate and had dealings with members of his own sex because we had talked about it many times during our school days and before he had left for Chicago. In fact, whenever Harold told me of an experience he had had with a man, I would listen attentively, amazed and excited. My knowledge was very limited, but I knew a little about the lives of gay people from Harold.

One morning in October, a letter from Harold arrived, saying that he was returning to New York because he was bored with Chicago and his family. A week later he arrived, called me, and we arranged to meet that evening. We talked about various things but mostly about Chicago.

"You've no idea how I hated it there, Tommy, my family always on my back. I couldn't wait to get out. I'm staying with my cousin and my younger brother, so there should be no problems."

2

Harold was a tall, black boy, a few months older than me, with light skin, broad lips, about six feet one inch tall, and weighed about 140 pounds.

We talked for a while longer, and I mentioned to Harold that at work there was a young boy I liked very much. From the way I spoke, Harold didn't take much time before he diagnosed my case (or so he said).

"Honey, sounds to me like you're in love with him."

"In love? Oh, Harold, don't be silly!" Of course, never having been in love, I really didn't know if it was true or not, but being in love with another boy sounded silly to me.

"Silly?" he said, a slight smile crossing his broad lips. "Silly perhaps, but true nonetheless. I've been around gay life for quite some time now, Tom; and let's face it, you may not know it—or realize it—but from everything you've told me, you're gay, too. You're what is known as a closet queen; you just haven't come out yet! Look, baby, straight guys don't go around liking other guys as much as you like this Jim. Sure, they admire famous men to a certain extent, but it ends after a while, or they outgrow it. You've been feeling this way about him for too long a time now, which makes me feel you are in love with him but don't know it".

"But—" I started to speak but he interrupted me.

"Tom, I didn't mean to hurt you. I hope I haven't. I just thought you'd want the truth, as I think it is, rather than have me lie to you."

"Naturally, I want the truth, it's just that I haven't thought of anything like this, and it's so new and a bit confusing right now. But I must admit the thought of it is a bit exciting."

It seems this was what Harold was waiting for me to say, for he replied, "Look, find out for yourself, and if you don't like it, there's nothing lost, and you will have found a bit of yourself and perhaps some peace of mind as well."

"I don't follow you."

"Well, you told me you like dressing in women's clothes on Thanksgiving every year, right?"

"Yes, but—"

"But nothing. Each year, in Harlem, there's a dance given by a club, and every drag queen in town will attend. Drag is what you do on Thanksgiving, honey. Anyone who's anyone in gay life will be there. If you haven't anything to wear, we can work on it and get you something. Would you like to go?"

"Gee, Harold, I don't know. Let me think about it, and I'll call you."

"Okay, but I wish you would. I'm sure you'd love it."

After I left him and went home, I did think about what he had said and was frightened at the thought of appearing in public in women's clothes. I was also excited and didn't know why. It was something new; nonetheless, I called Harold back and told him I would go.

"Wonderful! I'll call you during the week, and we'll meet and make arrangements. There are some people I want you to meet, and they're going, too."

A week or so later, I was introduced to Harold's immediate crowd, and discussions for the forthcoming drag began. There were three Puerto Rican boys: one named Pat and one named Alan, who were about sixteen years old, and a third named Terry, who was Alan's cousin and about two years older than Harold and me, although he didn't look it. They talked about different things, most of which I didn't fully understand, and I tried hard to piece it together.

As I watched the others being fitted for their outfits, Alan became quite friendly. Before long, I was sitting on the edge of the bed talking with him.

"You're awfully cute, Tom," he said.

"Am I?" I asked, and he moved closer.

"Yes, real cute," and kissed me fully on the mouth, just as Harold entered the room.

"Say, what's going on here? Now, really Miss Devlin, you are quite the one, aren't you?" I blushed (in those days I blushed at everything) and got up. I was speechless, although, in all honesty, I did enjoy it, and it made me feel wanted. The others just laughed, and the incident was forgotten as quickly as it had started.

When we left, Harold asked how I liked his friends.

"Oh, they seem like a nice bunch of kids, and Terry is so funny. I couldn't stop laughing."

"Yes, he has that way about him. Takes everything with a grain of salt, but don't let him fool you, Tom, he's the most sincere and serious one in the crowd."

"I don't doubt that for a minute, Harold."

Needless to say, the following weeks were spent in preparation for the big night. With Harold's help, I purchased a pair of high-heel shoes and a white wig used primarily for an old woman's Halloween costume. Trying to curl it with a hot curling iron was impossible. In my bathroom, late at night and alone, private rehearsals were going on. I cut bangs and placed a scarf around my head, tying it under the nape of my neck at the rear. Thinking it looked well and I was a sensation, I decided I would wear it that way the night of the dance. I couldn't have been more wrong if I had planned it. I also took one of my mother's dresses, which was too large for me, but with a belt and pulled in here and there it was, I thought, passable.

After having Thanksgiving dinner, I told my parents I was going to a dance and left for Harold's cousin's house. After redressing, the five of us, Terry, Pat, Alan, Harold, and I took the subway to the dance. The looks from the people were both frightening and, at times, amusing. Looking back, I suppose we were something of a sight ourselves, or, rather, something to figure out.

When we arrived at the dance, there was a huge crowd outside lined up on each side of the entrance to the ballroom.

Wooden police horses kept the people back. As we entered, the crowd would shout and scream their approval or disapproval of the outfits worn by those entering. When I saw the crowd, I became quite nervous and wanted to go home.

"Don't worry, Tom, this goes on all the time. Just smile at them, but, for Pete's sake, don't open your mouth. I know you when you get mad; you've got a tongue that waggles for days."

"I won't, I'm too scared!"

Inside the ballroom, the dance floor was already crowded with people. Boys danced with boys, girls with girls, boys with girls, costumed people, any and all combinations were dancing and walking around, talking and drinking. A line formed inside the dance floor on either side of the entrance doors, so that everyone could be seen as they arrived. Greetings were shouted across the room.

"Hi, Mae, ya look gorgeous! Where'd you get the drag?"

"Sweetie, you're a knockout. Never saw you look more lovely!"

Comments such as these were heard throughout the evening. From time to time, we went to the bar for a drink. Terry and I danced most of the evening, he following, me leading, such as it was. Later, as Terry and I were dancing, I looked around and saw two boys from my office in their own clothes dancing together. To their left was a girl who also worked with them. Thinking they would recognize me, I told Terry what had happened, and before he had time to answer, I was off the dance floor and over to a corner.

He came over and said, "What are you afraid of? If they're here, they're either gay or at least wise. There's no reason to be frightened."

"I know, Terry, but just the same, I'd rather they didn't see me."

"Okay, but come back. Just keep away from them."

Since there were so many people at the dance, losing them

wasn't hard. We went back to the dance floor as the announcement was made that the Grand March was about to begin. As only Harold was entering, we stood by and watched the parade of costumes and drags march across the stage to the cheering and whistling of the crowd. There were some really beautiful outfits, and to distinguish some of them from real women was almost impossible. Others were quite obviously boys in women's attire, but, for the most part, the majority of the contestants looked like women, and, in some cases, better.

After Harold had paraded across the stage, he was helped down the few steps by a uniformed guard. As he started down, the heel of his shoe caught on the step, and he fell right into the arms of the policeman. The people nearby let out a roar, and fortunately he wasn't hurt. He came over laughing and slightly limping.

"Did you see the grand exit I just made? I thought I'd die of embarrassment!"

"That's what you get for trying to be such a lady." Alan said, smiling.

Just before the parade ended, Harold suggested that we leave because the police protection was lifted at midnight, and he wanted to be far away by then. We didn't want to go home yet and took the subway to Forty-second Street, went into a penny arcade, and took pictures. When Harold saw mine, he said he would like to have it. I didn't particularly like it, so I gave it to him.

A short time later, we returned to Harold's cousin's house and changed our clothes. About 1:00 A.M. I dragged myself home. Next day at work I was completely exhausted and thankful it was the end of the week.

TWO

The following Friday night, Harold asked me to go to the Village with him, reminding me not to forget my ID card. I had never been there, and I arranged to meet Terry and him at 11:00 P.M. We took the subway to Eighth Street, walked about two blocks, and entered a small but neat bar on Eighth Street called Main Street. The long, straight bar was on the left as you entered, with a partition separating the tables on the right-hand side. The bar was very crowded and contained mostly young men. Only a few women were seated at the end of the bar. We pushed our way to the rear and after getting our drinks, stood by the jukebox. Since this was Harold's favorite bar, he knew many people and began introducing me to his friends. They all seemed very pleasant, and I immediately felt very much at ease. I had been tense when we first entered, but now that had vanished. At the end of the evening, as we were on our way home, Harold asked me how I had enjoyed myself.

"I had a wonderful time. It wasn't at all like I pictured it to be, and the people were so very nice. When are we going again?"

"Whenever you like," he said. "Tomorrow night?"

"Yes, I'd love to!"

"Okay, then, we'll meet at the same time and place. If anything should come up to change our plans, we'll call each other."

The next evening, we were back at the bar again. Being a Saturday night, it was more crowded than the night before. After ordering drinks, we positioned ourselves again near the jukebox and began talking with some of the people we had met the night before. About a half hour later, a young man came over to play some records. He asked me what I would like to hear.

"Nothing special, but if they have any Latin music, I'd like to hear that."

He made a few selections, and we began talking. His name was Paul, and he was from Connecticut. He told me he only came to the city on weekends. He began buying me drinks and, although I didn't realize it, was trying to proposition me. When he finally came out and told me what he wanted, I became a bit upset and nervous. I tried to think of a way to decline without hurting him, but this was new to me, and I didn't know what to do. I excused myself and went over to talk to Harold and Terry, telling them what Paul had said.

"Just tell him you're sorry, but you're really much too tired and will see him next week. If he's that interested, it'll work," said Harold.

I went back and told Paul what Harold had instructed me to say. He was a bit disappointed and asked if there was anything he could do to change my mind.

"I'm afraid not. I'm sorry."

"Well, will you be here next weekend, Tom?" he asked.

"I think so!"

"Good, then I'll look forward to seeing you then!" He said good night and left.

I felt more at ease after he left, and just before the bar closed Terry, Harold, and I went for coffee.

"Are you beginning to get the swing of things, Tom?" asked Terry.

"No, not exactly. I suppose it will take time. I just don't want to go home with the first person I meet, but who knows? We'll see what happens."

At work my friendship with Jim continued as usual, although I didn't mention my new interests to him nor did I think he would be interested. A week or so after meeting Paul, I took him to a friend of Harold's apartment. There I was really introduced for the first time to relations with a man, although, I must admit, they were very limited. I did very little, and when it was over, I was satisfied, but I was sure Paul wasn't, although he didn't say anything. He was, as usual, very polite, and said he would see me the following week in the bar and left. After he left, I returned to bed and went to sleep. I had told my parents I would be staying over at a friend's house that night.

The weekends that followed brought our trio to my now favorite bar. In fact, it was the only bar I knew, but it didn't seem to bother me. Christmas was coming, which I loved, and things in general seemed fine. I saw Paul several times, but we never got together other than that first night. Harold jokingly called me the "Queen of the Bar" because, for some reason, no matter how crowded it was, someone at the very end of the bar would get up and give me a seat, facing the entrance, so I could see everyone who came and went. (Again, for some reason, this practice of getting a seat has been with me all of my life—and I was only nineteen at the time—strange, isn't it?)

About a week before Christmas, I was standing in the rear of the bar, talking with some people. I looked over near the service section and saw the two boys who worked in my building whom I had seen at the Thanksgiving dance, George Jennings and Jerry Leighman. At first they didn't see me, but as they turned around after ordering their drinks, they noticed me and came over.

"Well, fancy meeting you here," said George.

"I always *thought* you were gay," chimed Jerry.

"Well, at least we have someone to talk with at work," added George. "How long have you been coming here?"

"A couple of weeks now. I love it! I've met some of the nicest people here," I told them.

"Don't count on it," warned George. "Some of them are

smart cookies and are only interested in one thing. Just be careful and watch your step. You're still new to all this, so take it easy."

"I will, George, and thanks for the advice."

"Well, we better be running along now, we have a few more places uptown we want to hit before closing. See you Monday," said George, and they left the bar.

After they left, I asked Harold what the uptown bars were like.

"You wouldn't like them, Tom, they're much too phony. Most of the guys walk around with their noses in the air and the attitude that they're so much better than you, which, of course, they aren't."

"Oh, Harold, I can't believe there are places like that. Let's go some night."

"Not me, I've had my fill of it. You can go if you want to, but I'm staying here in the Village, where I feel safe and where I belong."

"Have Terry and the others been there?"

"Sure they have!"

"And do they like them?"

"Terry can take it or leave it; he circulates a lot. Why don't you ask him to take you some night?"

"I will!"

I left Harold and went over to where Terry was standing. "Am I interrupting anything?"

"No, not at all."

"Terry, Harold tells me you go to the uptown bars quite often. What are they like?"

"Not much different from any other bar, or, for that matter, this one. Why?"

"Because I've heard about them, and this is the only bar I known and I'd like to spread out, so to speak, and see what the others are like. Can we go some time?"

"Sure. When would you like to go?"

"Whenever you say."

"How about after the New Year; start it right!"

"Swell!"

Our conversation having ended, I left him alone to cruise and returned to the others. Again, before the bar closed we made our usual trip for coffee and hamburgers and then home.

New Year's Eve found us back at Main Street. It was more crowded than ever. During the course of the evening, I was invited to a party at a nearby hotel. Not wanting to go alone, I went over to some friends and asked them what I should do.

"By all means, go! The guy that invited you knows loads of people. You'll have a ball, and besides, it's New Year's Eve, so have a happy one, baby."

A while later, a group of us left for the party. When we arrived, the party was well underway, and almost everyone was already drunk or at least a bit high, myself included. This was my first gay party, and I wanted to enjoy every minute of it. Later, as I started for the bathroom with a drink in my hand, I found a line outside the door. *Just like the bar.* I smiled to myself and took my place in line. When my turn came to go in, the man who invited me to the party pushed his way in with me. I put the drink on the floor and urinated, feeling uneasy with this stranger so close to me. When I finished, he turned me around and kissed me. The feeling aroused me, and, before I knew it, his hands were examining my body. Finding their way to the desired spot, he freed me and further freed the passion that was now burning within me. When it was over, he thanked me, and we both left the bathroom. The line outside had gotten quite long, and comments were thrown at us as we passed. He just smiled, and we continued to the living room to join the others. The evening from that point on went smoothly, and some time in the early morning of 1950 I found my way home and fell, exhausted, into bed.

THREE

The uptown bars, as Terry had predicted, weren't different from Eighth Street. Some were very large, others small. One bar I liked in particular was in the West Seventies. Everyone seemed friendly, and I liked the atmosphere immediately. Terry liked it, too. For weeks we went there, and I couldn't imagine why Harold disliked uptown bars. *Oh, well,* I thought, *to each his own.*

One Sunday evening Terry took me to a dance in Harlem. It was a weekly affair held on the top floor of an old building. Inside the large, dimly lit room were tables and chairs all around the dance floor. In the back was a small bar that served beer and Cokes. A three-piece band screeched out almost unrecognizable tunes as boys danced together.

Terry knew some people, and after introductions were made, we joined them. Before the night was over, I learned, without too much difficulty, to follow rather than lead in dancing.

For three months we frequented various bars and on Sundays the dance. One Sunday afternoon in April, I called Terry and asked him if he was going to the dance that evening.

"I don't think so. Not tonight, I'm too tired."

"Oh, come on, never can tell who you might meet! This might be your lucky night. Besides, you know how I hate going alone."

"No, Tom, I don't think I should."

"Please, pretty please with sugar," I coaxed.

"Well, since you put it that way, okay, though it's against

my better judgment. And there better be someone there for me, or else," he said laughingly.

"Okay, meet you at nine, usual place."

At the dance we took a table in the rear of the room near the little bar. As the evening went on we danced with each other and with different guys who came over and asked us to dance. At one point, I was sitting alone having a cigarette and a drink while Terry was dancing. Two boys I didn't know sat down at the end of the long table. They were talking in tones loud enough for me to hear, although I wasn't paying too much attention. Their conversation was general. The tallest of the two, who was quite attractive with a moustache and small beard, asked his friend, who was Puerto Rican and also very attractive, who the blonde at the end of the table was. I didn't think they were talking about me and was surprised when the Puerto Rican boy turned to me and said, "Hi, my name is Bill Lopez, what's yours?"

"Tom!" I blurted out. "Tom Devlin!"

"Tom, this is Ray."

We exchanged greetings and then Ray said, "You're very quiet tonight, Tom. Is anything wrong?"

"No, I'm usually quiet."

"Are you here alone?" he asked.

"No, I'm here with a friend. He's dancing now," I said, pointing to Terry on the dance floor.

"Oh, Terry, yes, I know him very well. He's a wonderful person."

"Yes, he is!"

"Would you like to dance, Tom?"

"Yes, I'd love to."

As we got up to dance, I noticed Bill looking at us. *My, but he's cute,* I thought. *Wish he'd ask me to dance.*

When we finished our dance and returned to the table, Terry had joined us. The band played a slow tune, and Bill asked me to dance. We danced together for the rest of the evening, and when the dance was over, he took me home. He lived not too far from where I did. He asked for my phone number, which I was only too happy to give, and promised to call the following evening at seven o'clock. Bill was about my height and weight, with wavy dark hair, almost black, black eyes, and long eye-lashes. His olive complexion and clean-cut features made him a truly handsome young man. He was one month to the day younger than me, and I would be twenty in June and he in July.

The next evening he called, and we went to a movie, then to Harold's house. We necked and held each other, and I felt wonderful. I had never felt this way about any one I had met so far, and the feeling was beautiful. All I knew was that I enjoyed being with him, and he seemed to enjoy being with me. As the evening ended, he promised to call, and I couldn't wait to see him again.

We saw each other every day after that but were never alone sexually as neither of us had an apartment. Finally, one day he told me he was going to get an apartment in Manhattan with a friend of his. Living at home had its advantages, and even though his parents knew he was gay, he still wanted to be on his own. This seemed a good idea to me, too, because then I could spend nights at his house without my parents worrying were I was, and I was longing to be alone with him in bed.

Not too much time was spent in apartment hunting, and Bill took the first half-way decent place he found. One evening, I met him at the movie theater he worked in, and he introduced me to the young man who was to be his future roommate. His name was Joe Davidson. He was over six feet tall, had light red hair that was cut short, and his clear, blue green eyes seemed to have a hard quality to them. He was dressed very neatly in a black suit.

"Tom, this is Joe, Joe, this is my lover, Tom," said Bill.

"Hi," said Joe and turned his back to me and continued talking with Bill.

I felt hurt and immediately disliked Joe. *He's going to be Bill's roommate,* I thought to myself, *and he doesn't like me. I'll probably be seeing almost as much of him as Bill, so what do I do?* I told myself I had to speak to Bill about this after he got off work that night.

When Bill finished work that evening, we met for dinner in a restaurant around the corner from the theater. I told him I didn't think that Joe liked me, and it was bothering me.

"Don't mind him. He's like that. Doesn't mean a thing, just that he doesn't know you yet. When he does, I'm sure he'll love you almost as much as I do—well, maybe not as much, but you know what I mean, hon."

"I hope so, Bill."

The apartment consisted of one large room on the top floor, facing the street. It was on West Eighty-second Street, a very quiet block close to Riverside Drive. Two single day-beds were situated against one wall, with a chest of drawers separating them. A large chair, a kitchen table, two chairs, and a sink completed the room. The bathroom was in the hall and was shared by three other tenants.

The first night I stayed over, we were lucky enough to be alone, as Joe had decided to spend the night at his parents' home in New Jersey. This was to be my first time alone with Bill, and the anticipation was great. After we listened to some records, had a drink or two, we started making love. He began kissing every inch of my body, and I was almost ready to explode. From my lips, he continued to my neck, shoulders, nipples, and down to the navel. He continued his travel along that path until he reached my already rigid manhood. Immediately, he was on it, and I could hardly contain myself. I may have been new, but I wanted to please Bill, and so I did whatever he did to me to him.

"You'd better take it easy. I can't take it much longer," I whispered, but it was too late for both of us.

He reversed his pattern, and made his way back from where he was to my lips, which he kissed for what seemed an eternity. A short time later, we fell asleep in each other's arms.

Joe and I started getting along fairly well. On the nights he was at home when Bill wanted to make love, I felt a bit strange because I knew he was awake and listening. Bill assured me he was a heavy sleeper, but I had my doubts. As it turned out, he was indeed a heavy sleeper.

April and May went by quickly. With June and the warm weather, we started going to a beach in Long Island on weekends. It was a lovely beach, very quiet and secluded. Naturally, Bill knew many people and introduced me. One boy in particular to whom I took an immediate liking was named Frank DeSal. He was Italian, about an inch shorter than me, and very thin. He had dark hair and was rather sexy looking. I didn't swim, and since Bill did, he was in the water a good part of the afternoon. It was during this time that Frankie and I struck up a conversation. He told me he was very unhappy because he had just broken up with a lover of two years named Tony. As he spoke, I felt sorry for him. He was a very handsome boy and really shouldn't have had any problems, but obviously he was still very much in love with this Tony. We found we had many mutual interests, and I wanted to see him again. Not sexually, but I wanted him as a good friend.

As I was thinking this, Bill came out of the water. "Hey, what are you two so engrossed in?" he asked.

"Nothing, Bill, Frankie was just telling me about Tony."

"Yes, Frank, how is Tony?" asked Bill.

"Haven't you heard? We broke up—again."

"You mean this isn't the first time?" I interrupted.

"Hell, no, it's been an off-again, on-again romance since we met. I suppose I should be used to it by now, but every time it happens, it's like the first time all over again, although this time it looks like it's the last," Frankie said sadly.

"Don't be so sure, Frank," said Bill. "Knowing Tony the way I do, he'll be back, and you'll take him back, and it'll all be as if nothing happened."

"I hope you're right, Bill—I really hope so," Frankie said, looking at him.

"Well, kids, it's getting late; we better start for home," Bill said.

We decided that rather than taking the bus back to the train station, we would try and hitch a car ride. A car pulled up about one hundred feet from us and we ran to get in. As the car sped along the road, I suddenly remembered I had left my blanket and bathing suit on the road where we had been standing.

"Oh, hell, there goes another suit. I won't be able to come out here much longer, Bill, at the rate I'm losing things. This is the third one this summer. I either loan them out, leave them some place, or some other dumb thing."

"Well, if you weren't in such a hurry, you wouldn't have forgotten it." Bill smiled.

"Shut up," I snapped, smiling at him.

As the weeks passed we saw much of each other and the beach. Now that the summer was well under way, the topic of conversation was vacation. We decided to take our vacation in Provincetown, on Cape Cod. We had heard about it from many people who had been there, and everyone seemed to love the place. I had never been on a vacation, and I began looking forward to it. My first vacation, my first lover, new friends: it all seemed so wonderful! I couldn't wait until the first week in July when we would be on our way

FOUR

We arranged to meet at the bus depot early in the evening. We knew it would be a long trip and thought we would sleep on the bus. There were five of us going: Bill and I, Johnny and Nicky (two boys I had met at Main Street when I first started going there and who were lovers), and Terry. Since the rest of us were couples, this left poor Terry the only single in the crowd, but somehow he didn't seem to mind.

The bus ride seemed endless. Nine hours after we left New York we arrived in Provincetown. It was early morning, and not many people were up. We looked for a place to stay and finally took a three-room cottage at the end of town. It consisted of two bedrooms, a bath, and kitchen. One bedroom was shared by Johnny and Nicky; the other, which had two beds, was shared by Bill, Terry, and I. Johnny later suggested that it would be cheaper for everyone if we all chipped in and bought food at the supermarket, and, since he was a good cook, we all agreed he would do the cooking. It was also agreed that each of us would take turns doing the dishes. After shopping and returning to the cottage, we had lunch and went on a short sight-seeing tour of the town.

In the evening, after a wonderful meal prepared by Johnny, and the dishes having been finished, we all took our turns showering and getting ready to go out. Johnny had been to "P Town" before and knew all the places to go. We walked down the main street and window shopped for awhile and then entered a bar Johnny told us about.

It was called the "A House." It was small with many sea objects hanging from the ceiling and walls. To the right as we entered was a small square inlet with tables and chairs for about ten or fifteen people. On the wall above the tables was painted a picture of the town's wharf. We ordered our drinks and were fortunate to find a table. Terry decided not to join us and in a flash disappeared into the crowd. The four of us sat quietly talking and drinking, and I felt great. Here I was on my first vacation with someone I really loved and who loved me, and everything seemed so right. It was like a dream, and I didn't want to wake up. I was still in this frame of mind when we came home at the end of the evening, and Bill and I made love. We were lucky that Terry did not come home that evening.

The beach was wonderful—long, clean, and beautifully white. The water was so clear you could see to the bottom. I watched as Terry dove in and swam around for what seemed like hours. He called me at one point and said, "Tommy, watch this—the only Esther Williams," (referring to the lovely swimming star of MGM pictures), and he started doing backstrokes ever so gracefully. Bill and I laughed and told him we were going to take a walk. We started along the shore and from time to time splashed water on each other. The sun was very hot, and I was beginning to get a bit red. When we returned to our blanket, I put on a shirt so I wouldn't get too burned.

On the way home from the beach, we stopped at a restaurant that was located halfway between the beach and the town. It was called "The Moors" and was quite large and typical of everything we had seen. It was in keeping with the decor of the rest of the town, and, being a fishing village, most of the restaurants, shops, etc., had something depicting the sea.

"I've heard so much about this place," said Terry. "Someone told me this is where everyone goes in the afternoon after the beach for cocktails between four and five o'clock. They say they have community singing here, and it's supposed to be a ball."

He had no sooner said this than the place began to fill up. We ordered drinks and sandwiches, and at four o'clock the piano started up, and the singing began. We really had a good time. After the hour was over, we returned to the cottage, without Terry. He had told me earlier, "You go on ahead, I think there's a number interested in me and, believe me, I am in him, so don't wait for me." Obviously he did meet his friend because he didn't show up for dinner that evening.

For the next three days the schedule was much the same: breakfast, beach, The Moors for cocktails, home, cleanup, dinner, and then out for the evening. I was happy as a lark. However, on the fourth day I began to notice that Bill was acting strangely.

"Is anything wrong?" I asked. "You've been acting strangely."

"No, hon, nothing's wrong. Just my way, you know that."

I didn't give the matter much more thought, and later that evening when were sitting drinking at the A House, Bill started talking to an older man at the next table. Their conversation was too low for me to hear, what with the noise from the jukebox and people in the bar. Johnny and Nicky had already gone home, and Terry was somewhere in the back of the bar, which left Bill and me alone at the table. Then, suddenly, as if I were a casual acquaintance, Bill announced in a voice loud enough for several others nearby to hear that he was going home with the older man. I couldn't believe my ears.

"What do you mean you're going home with him? What the hell am I supposed to do?"

"That's your problem," he said. "I'll see you later," and he and the man left the bar. I sat there, not fully aware of what was happening and, with tears in my eyes, slowly got up and looked for Terry. I found him and told him what had happened.

"You're kidding!" he said, really surprised.

All I could do was nod.

"You mean they just got up and left you sitting there?"

"Yes."

"Come on, honey, I'm taking you home. We'll get to the bottom of this."

When we arrived at the cottage, Johnny and Nicky were asleep and Bill hadn't come in yet. Terry suggested we have coffee and wait for Bill.

"No, I don't want any. I'm going to bed," I said, still shaken.

"Well, okay, you run along. I'll just have a cup and a cig and hit the sack myself. I think I'll sleep on the couch tonight in case Bill does come home. I'm sure you'll have plenty to talk about," he said.

"Thanks, Terry. I appreciate it."

I woke some time later when I heard a car stop in front of our cabin. There was a moment of silence, and then I heard someone enter the cabin. Seconds later, Bill was standing in the doorway to the bedroom. His hair was messed, and he reeked of liquor. I stared at him for a minute and then turned and faced the wall. Resting my head on the pillow, I began to cry softly.

"Have fun, Bill?" I asked bitterly. "Was he better than me? He should be, he's older and probably has a hell of a lot more experience."

"Look, Tom, nothing happened, but it could have. I said no. We're just having dinner together tomorrow night."

"And what the hell am I supposed to do in the meantime?" I asked.

"I don't know why the hell you're so upset, Tom. All I did was go out and have a good time. You're always complaining that we have to watch our money. Well, I'm fed up with you and your pleading poverty. I want someone to spend money on me, and if this guy wants to do it, I'm not going to stop him."

I couldn't believe my ears. If trying to save money for both of us was "pleading poverty," then I guess I was guilty, although I wasn't aware of it. It was the first time he had mentioned anything like this, and I was shocked.

"What do you want me to do, support you? Well, if I could, I would, and you know it."

"No, I don't want you to support me, but I'm sick and tired of hearing about how little money you have. I think it would be best if we went our separate ways," he said, looking down at the floor.

"You don't mean that. Why, Bill, why? Why should a thing like money have anything to do with us? You said you loved me: well, you know that I certainly love you. Why isn't that enough?" I was now in tears.

"It isn't enough, Tom. You don't understand how I feel. Sure I love you, but we can't go on together any longer. It's just one of those things, and I can't explain it. Sure I want love, but I also want something more out of life, and I'm going to try and get it the best way I can. You're still new to this life, you'll find someone who'll love you. Don't waste your time on me; I'm not worth it."

"You *are* worth it, Bill, to me." The tears came freely now, and I didn't try to hide them as before.

"Don't cry, Tom, you know I can't stand to see you cry. It'll take a little time, but you'll get over it."

"No, Bill, I won't. I love you so very much. I don't know what I'll do without you or how I managed before we met."

"Don't talk like that, it's pure nonsense."

"No, it's not. How can you say you love me and then in the same breath say that we can't be together? I just don't understand, Bill, I just don't understand."

"Let's not talk about it anymore tonight, Tom. I'm tired."

"An easy way out, huh, Bill?"

"No, I'm not trying to get out of anything, but at this rate we're not going to settle anything by a lot of talking, especially this late at night. Things will be different in the morning. I'm going to bed."

He started for the bathroom. I was sitting on the edge of the bed, tears slowly coming down my cheeks. *What did I do wrong?* I kept thinking. *I can't let him go, I love him too much. I must get him back, somehow, some way—but how? What am I going to do?* (At this point I felt like Vivien Leigh in *Gone with the Wind*—similar dialogue, but for me a very serious problem.)

When he returned from the bathroom, I was facing the wall. He got into bed quietly and whispered good night. It hurt and hurt very much, but he was next to me now, even though I knew nothing would happen. How I longed to have him hold me. I kept thinking about what he said and softly cried myself to sleep.

He kept his dinner date the following night and went out almost nightly with various people for the rest of the week. I hardly saw him. Each night would bring another argument. Seeing him with other people only arose the jealousy in me. Bill tried to give the impression that he could care less, but I knew it bothered him. What I didn't know was that he thought this was the best way to make me realize our affair was over. He wanted a variety of affairs and yet a steady one. Of course, he knew this was impossible, although he would try and have it as long as he could.

With the Fourth of July over and the week as well, we decided to take the boat back to Boston and the bus from there to New York. The people we met during the week came to the pier to say their farewells, as well as others who were seeing their "lovers for a week" off. There were tears of loneliness in some of the boys' eyes, since they knew full well that they might never see their lovers for a week again. I had tears, too, but for a different reason. My relationship hadn't lasted just a week, but four wonderful months. Admittedly not very long, but it was a little different for me.

On the boat back I sat and thought of all the things that had happened during the last four months, while Bill spent his time at the bar. On the bus later, he slept. I tried but couldn't. When we arrived in New York, Bill said he would call the next day. He didn't! He called about a week later, but there was no change in his attitude. During this time, I didn't want to go out or see anyone, I felt so lonesome and mixed up. Occasionally I would go to a movie with Pat or Terry, but that was the extent of it. Bill called one evening to tell me that Joe had lost his job and was moving back to his parents' house in New Jersey, and he was moving back for a while with his parents in the Bronx.

One evening Bill called and asked me to come over. His parents were out, and he wanted to talk. I don't know what I expected, but when I arrived at his house, the first thing he said was, "Tommy, I want us to be friends. I'll always love you, you know that, but it's different now—a different kind of love, and a very special, wonderful kind of love, fresh and clean. Don't spoil it, please."

"I know, Bill, and I want to keep it that way, too. Yes, I still love you, but I see now it's useless."

Then he told me of his new interest, and that he wanted me to meet David. I dreaded the thought but knew it was inevitable. He played some records. One was a new dance called the Mambo, which I had heard but couldn't do.

"Come on, I'll teach you," he said and pulled me up from the couch.

And teach me he did! By the time I left that evening, we were experts in this new dance craze.

Several weeks later, while sitting in booth with some friends at the Verdi Bar on West Seventy-second Street, Bill came in. He stopped by to say hello, and my heart jumped. After the usual small talk, he said to me, "When you get a chance, come in the back, I want you to meet David."

"David?" I said, not recalling his mentioning him a few weeks earlier.

"Yes, the boy I was telling you about. He's so nice, Tom, I'm sure you're going to like him. I've told him all about you, and he's dying to meet you."

Downing a few more drinks for courage, I went back to meet Bill's new friend. When I arrived at the table, they were sitting alone. Bill made the introductions and ordered drinks.

"Bill has told me so many nice things about you, Tom. I was really looking forward to meeting you. And, if I may say so, he was wrong."

"Wrong about what?" I inquired.

"You're much nicer than he said."

How could you dislike a person after a compliment like that? I said to myself. He was nice. He was Mexican, and, although not extremely handsome, there was something about him that was appealing. "Thank you, David, it's a pleasure meeting you, too."

We talked for about fifteen minutes, and David asked me to dinner the following Friday at his house. I told him I'd love to.

"Good! Bill will call and give you the time and address. Again, Tom, it's been a pleasure, and I'll look forward to seeing you Friday."

"Thank you, and thanks for the drink. I'll be there."

They left, and after they did, I thought to myself, *Well, at least Bill is with a nice person.* I returned to my table and ordered another drink.

FIVE

Bill called during the week and told me David was called out of town on business, but our dinner date was still on if I was interested. I said yes since I wanted to see David's apartment anyway. He gave me the address, and I told him I would be over after work on Friday.

After a short tour of the two-room apartment, we had dinner and listened to records.

"Love your hair, Tom. When did you do it?" he asked.

"During the week! I was so damn sick and tired of my mousy color I had to do something," I replied. "Do you really like it?"

"Love it! You know how I like blond hair, especially on you. But you had it once before, didn't you?"

"Yes, shortly before I met you. I usually keep it for awhile, get tired, let it grow back, get bored again, and dip it again. You know me."

"I sure do; but it looks great."

"Thanks."

"Want to hear anything special?" he asked.

"You know me, anything Latin; I still love it."

"Okay, as a matter of fact, David brought back some from Mexico on his last trip. They aren't too bad; a bit hillbilly, if you don't mind that sort of thing."

"No, doesn't bother me."

We listened to the records, and he said, "Tom, I can talk to you freely, can't I? I mean, we're friends. No hard feelings?"

"Of course not. What's wrong?"

"Nothing's terribly wrong, just that at times I don't trust David. Some of the things he says and does just don't add up. I can't explain it exactly; you'd have to experience it for yourself."

"Bill, I'm the last person to advise you or anyone, for that matter, on the subject of love. I still don't know my ass from a hole in the wall, so don't depend on me for advice, although I appreciate your thoughtfulness in asking for it. We couldn't get along together, so how can I possibly advise anything?"

"Tom, he tells me he loves me, but I'm doubtful."

"You said you loved me once, too. Aren't the tables turned a little?" I asked.

"I did love you, Tom, and still do in my own way, but this is different. The way you felt about me, I feel about David. Oh, I'm so mixed-up lately. Sometimes I wish we were still together."

My heart almost stopped as he spoke. *Could there still be a chance?* I thought. *No, why be foolish? It's over, and I'm better off forgetting it. Why should I be hurt any more than I am?*

After he spoke, he leaned over and kissed me tenderly. I was surprised at his action, and we just sat looking at each other for a few minutes.

"I'm sorry, Tom. I just felt like doing that. I'm so sorry, please forgive me!"

"Don't worry about it, I didn't think anything of it," I lied.

He suggested we take in a movie and turned the phonograph off. We got our coats and left the quiet of the small apartment.

My nights became a regular schedule, especially on weekends. I was beginning to become what my friends called a "barfly." *True,* I thought, *but then I haven't that many friends so why not go to the bars and meet people?* I loved it, and yet I hated it.

On a Friday night a few weeks later I was leaving the bar

with some friends when I heard someone call my name. When I looked around, I saw a middle-aged man wearing glasses walking toward me.

"Tommy?" he said. "You are Tommy Devlin, aren't you?"

"Yes," I replied, still somewhat confused as to who this man was and how he knew both my first and last names.

"I'm Ernest Locker, Bill Lopez's friend. I'm sure Bill has spoken to you about me."

"Oh yes, Ernest, he has," I replied. Bill had indeed told me about Ernest and about their affair. They had known each other before I met Bill and had gone on vacation to Jamaica together. I knew that Ernest paid for Bill's favors, but to what extent I didn't know. I also knew that Bill was getting money from some place and would take me out. Now I realized where that money came from.

"I'd like to talk to you, Tom, if I may, for just a few minutes," he said.

"Well, Ernest, I don't know. I'm very tired and it's late, and I should be getting home," I answered, hoping to get out of whatever it was he had in mind.

"Well, I have my car here. Suppose I drop you off at the subway? I'm going uptown anyway. Can't hurt you know!"

"No, I suppose it can't. Okay, you've got yourself a passenger." I said good night to my friends and started walking with Ernest to his car.

In the car, he tried to be very friendly, and I sensed this. "I realize you must hate me, Tom," he said, "but really you can't blame me for liking Bill. He's so damn good-looking. I can imagine the stories he must have told you about me."

"Ernest, I don't hate you, or anyone, for that matter, and I agree he is a very good-looking man. That, I think, is his whole problem."

"Tom, would you like to stop at my place and see some of the pictures we took on our trip to Jamaica?" he asked finally.

"Frankly, Ernest, I don't think—" I began, but he interrupted me.

"Don't worry, no strings attached. We can have a few drinks, and I'll drive you home later. How does that sound?"

"Okay, but not too late. I am a bit tired."

His apartment was small and neatly furnished. After we arrived, he told me to make myself at home and mixed drinks. He asked me what I would like, and I told him Bill had gotten me hooked on Jamaica Rum with Coke.

"Naturally," he smiled. "What else? In fact, I introduced him to that in Jamaica."

Another dig, I thought. I was beginning to get slightly bored, and yet this man strangely interested me—not sexually, but the way he spoke and carried himself, and since he was older, I felt a bit at ease with him. After he made the drinks, he brought out a large photograph album. As I glanced through it, he sat on the arm of the large chair I was sitting in and explained the pictures to me.

"This one was taken on the boat going over. There's Billy in the background trying hard to play tennis—what I think he was trying to do was make the tennis teacher," he said laughingly.

"And no doubt he did," I replied.

"No doubt, but I don't know for sure. Oh, here's one taken at night on the beach near Montego Bay. Good shot of him, isn't it?" I agreed.

He then told me he had been a minister in Jamaica for fourteen years before being transferred to the States and his present parish. I was naturally surprised because Bill had never mentioned the fact that Ernest was a minister. *Oh, well!* I thought.

The drinks were getting to me, and I thought better not to mention it. Although I was beginning to like Ernest, I didn't trust him. I also thought it best to call it a night and suggested I leave.

He drove me home, and as I was getting out of the car, I thanked him for everything.

"The pleasure was mine, Tommy, and please feel free to come over any time. My door is always open to you."

"Thank you very much. I'm very flattered! Well, good night."

The following Sunday afternoon, I received a call from a friend of Ernest. He told me that Ernest was having some people over and would like me to join them. I thanked the caller and told him I would be there.

When I arrived, there were about six or seven people in the apartment. Ernest made the introductions, and I sat in one of the large chairs facing the group. Two boys were dancing, two others were sitting on the bed deep in conversation, and the other three were sitting opposite me. They tried immediately to bring me into their conversation, which I appreciated.

"We haven't seen you here before," said the tallest of the three. "Have you known Ernest very long?"

"No, I haven't. As a matter of fact, we just met the other night."

"Boy, is he a fast worker," said a smiling blonde-haired boy to his friend. All I could do was blush and try to let it pass.

Ernest joined us with my drink and refills for the others. The conversation drifted from one topic to another, and then the tall boy asked me to dance. His name was Earl, and we danced most of the evening together. I was beginning to enjoy myself. After seven or eight drinks, I began necking with Earl. He told me Ernest was a bit upset because he was attracted to me. I said I liked Ernest but just as a friend. I also learned that Earl had been Bill's lover before he met me.

We made a date for dinner the following Friday night, exchanged phone numbers, and I told Ernest I had to leave because of work the following day. He offered to drive me home, but I felt it wasn't necessary and suggested he stay with his guests. He thanked me for coming while I thanked him for asking and said I had enjoyed myself. Sleepy and a bit high, I got home about 2:00 A.M. and went right to bed.

The following Friday, I met Earl for dinner. We went to a little bohemian restaurant in the Village. Very atmospheric! After dinner and drinks, we made a round of the bars, arriving late at my favorite uptown bar, which was also in Earl's neighborhood. We were sitting in a booth and talking quietly, when Bill entered the bar. He was surprised to see us together, and I thought the situation amusing, especially under the influence of liquor. Bill introduced his date and joined us.

"How's David?" I asked.

"Oh, didn't you know? We broke up a few months ago," he said.

"Sorry." I could have bitten my tongue. I hadn't known about it. and I'm sure he thought I was being bitchy. However, the evening seemed to fly by, and shortly Earl suggested we leave. We said our good-nights and went to his apartment, where he made coffee and put on some records. He asked if I wanted to hear anything special, and I told him no, as long as it was low and romantic. I was a bit surprised at myself for saying that, but I supposed the liquor was the answer. It wasn't long before Earl started making advances, to which I didn't object. He started kissing me softly, then passionately, and suggested we become one. Being quite high, I fell asleep and nothing happened.

In the morning after breakfast, we made a date for dinner that night. The same routine as the night before, only this time I made sure I was completely loaded with alcohol. When we arrived at his apartment and had a few more drinks, I was ready for him. This time I enjoyed it. When it was over, he whispered, "Perhaps we could do it again some time soon, Tom."

"I don't see why not. Perhaps we will."

We saw each other a few more times after that night, and it became a routine with us. I wasn't in love with Earl and didn't know how to tell him. Finally, we saw less and less of each other, and I continued to go out with other people.

SIX

A few days before Halloween, Harold called and invited me to a party along with Pat and Alan. He told us to come in drag as the people giving the party were gay girls and would love it. We dressed in the Village at Johnny and Nicky's apartment and took the subway to the party. We stayed there a few hours, and, since there weren't too many people, we decided to leave and go to a dance in the neighborhood. It was a Friday night, and the dance hall was crowded. Alan excused himself and went to sit in a booth with a trick he had met shortly after we arrived. Pat and I sat at a table and watched the floor show. The show was terrible, and we were starting to get bored. I was just about to suggest we leave, when Pat and I were pulled up from our chairs by two big men.

The place had been raided! The police let everyone who wasn't in drag go. There were about six or eight of us in drag, and the next thing we knew we were hauled off in a police van and whisked off to the nearest police station, which one I didn't and still don't know. After we were booked, each of us was assigned a separate cell. As I entered mine, the guard asked me for the belt to my dress. I asked him why, and he replied, "So you won't hang yourself, beautiful."

"I have nylons on if I want to do that," I said coldly.

I was frightened out of my mind, not knowing what was going to happen or how long we would be locked up. Alan was in the next cell to me and Pat next to him. Naturally we couldn't see each other, but after awhile I heard someone crying softly and asked who it was. Alan replied, "It's Pat. She's upset!"

"*She's* upset!" I answered. "What the hell do you think I am?"

"Oh, don't worry, they can't do anything to us," replied Alan, as if he had been through this before.

"But I am!" I answered.

"Well, honey, there's nothing you can do now. Just have to wait until morning and see what's up."

A while later I heard a noise from Alan's cell and asked what he was doing.

"Taking off my dress," he said. "I want to sleep and don't want to crease it."

Dizzy queen, I thought. *We're in jail, and all she can think about is her dress!*

In the morning we were again lined up, my belt having been returned and again put in the police van and transferred to the tombs downtown. As we were approaching the tombs, one of the drags, an older queen, took out her compact and began applying makeup. I asked her why and she replied, "Oh, there'll be photographers and reporters there, and I want to look my best, honey."

"Photographers!" I cried. "You're kidding!"

"No, dear, they're always around for something like this. We're news!"

That's all I needed to hear. I almost fainted on the spot. I could just see the headlines TOMMY DEVLIN ARRESTED IN WOMEN'S CLOTHES. What would my family say—and my job? I was in a state of near shock.

However, when we pulled up in front of the tombs, it was very quiet, and I was thankful that the queen had been just pulling my leg. I began to relax, but just a bit. I looked around quickly to make sure as I left the van and nearly fell on my face.

One of my heels got stuck on the steps as I was leaving the van, but I caught myself in time.

We were brought upstairs and placed in a large cell with about thirty or forty men of every type and description. Most of them were sitting on the benches that were around the cell. One black man got up and said to me, "You look as though you need a seat. Take mine." I thanked him and sat down. Alan and Pat stood close by.

We weren't there more than fifteen minutes when our names were called, and the three of us were taken to another large room just off the court proper. When we were left alone, I opened the door leading to the court and saw Terry and a friend of his sitting in the courtroom. How he knew about what had happened I didn't know, but just seeing him there made me feel a little better. He kept doing all sorts of facial motions until I finally got the message. He was trying to tell me to take off as much makeup as possible. I pulled off my hat, stuffed the small hairpiece into my purse, and with a tissue tried to wipe as much makeup off as I could. I must have looked ridiculous standing there in a lavender street length dress, light green topper, short blond hair, and little makeup.

We were finally called into the court to appear before the judge. He looked at us and asked, "What have we here?"

Since none of us could afford a lawyer, we assumed that the court had appointed one for us, and he answered, "They were at a Halloween dance, Your Honor."

To which the judge replied, "Well, it doesn't look as though they were ducking for apples to me."

Very funny, I thought to myself. The next thing I heard was the judge saying, "Fifty dollars' bail; hearing November 1."

Fifty dollars, I thought. *He might as well have said fifty thousand. Where am I going to get that kind of money?* I don't think between the three of us we had more than ten dollars. Again the panic began to rise in me. *Good God, I'm going to* have to stay in jail all week until the trial on Thursday. What will they say at home and at work? I now was almost near collapse from worry.

We were then led from the court down several staircases to another room where a guard was passing out clothes so that we could change. Alan and Pat began undressing, and I was just about to take off my dress when the guard called out, "Who's Devlin?"

"Me," I answered, tears flowing freely down my cheek.

"Come with me. You've been bailed out. Your friends are upstairs."

I told Alan and Pat not to worry, that I would do my best to raise the money and get them out, and left with the guard. When we arrived upstairs, Terry and his friend were waiting for me.

"Oh, Terry, I'm so happy to see you. Where did you get the money?"

"The owner of the dance bailed you out. We figured that Ernest would bail out Pat and Alan, but you're the one we were worried about. You have a job and have to be protected."

"How did you know about this?"

"You told Harold where you were going, and he decided to join you later. When he arrived he saw them taking you in and turned on his heels and flew home. He called me, and we checked, and, well, here we are!"

"And am I ever glad you are!"

As the guard was returning my personal belongings, he said to me, "You know, we can arrest you again the minute you set one foot on the sidewalk. You know that, don't you?"

When Terry heard this, he turned to me and said, "Wait here one minute," and with that he left the building. He returned a few minutes later, and we started to leave.

"Remember what I told you," repeated the cop. "The minute you put a foot on the sidewalk, we'll arrest you."

"If he puts a foot on the sidewalk!" replied Terry. With that both he and his friend lifted me by the arms and carried me to a waiting taxi.

After we arrived at Johnny's apartment, I changed and had breakfast. I was so glad to be out of jail that I swore I'd never go in drag again.

"Humm, I'll just bet," said Terry.

The following Thursday, with my hair flattened down and wearing a dark, conservative suit and tie, Alan, Pat, and I appeared in court for our trial. Ernest had been doing a little work on our behalf. Fortunately for us, he knew the chief of police from the district in which we were arrested. He told him that we had borrowed the clothes from girlfriends and had gone to a party on a lark. How we landed up at the dance he didn't know, but he assured him we were not homosexuals. Being a minister did have its points. The police chief naturally took his word and because of his testimony in court, the case was dropped, and we were released.

I couldn't believe it. We were free and didn't have a police record. The case had been thrown out of court, thanks to Ernest.

Things went along smoothly for the next few weeks, and as the Thanksgiving ball approached, I forgot my promise and decided to attend it, in drag, of course, in a store-bought, black, street-length dress, with a small cape that had tiny white daisies on the border. Not very chic, but much better than the year before; or, at least, I thought so.

During the course of the evening, I decided to use the men's room. As I approached, I spotted the detective that had arrested me standing near the entrance. I was panic-stricken for fear he would recognize me. Even though the dance was legal on Thanksgiving, I wanted no part of him. I then decided it was

time to leave and Pat, Alan, Terry, and I left and took the first
cab we found back to the Village and changed.

New Year's Eve of 1950–51 we spent at the Verdi Bar on
Seventy-second Street.

SEVEN

I had received notice from the Selective Service in January of 1951 to report for my army physical in early March. Strangely enough, Bill was to report the same day. When I arrived at Whitehall Street, I saw many of the guys with whom I had gone to grammar and high school. Many of them had changed greatly, gotten heavier, some of them almost unrecognizable. One of the questions on the written examination asked if the applicant were homosexual, to which I replied, "Tendencies!" Another asked, "Were you ever arrested?" to which I answered, "Yes," even though the charges had been thrown out. When one of the sergeants read this, he told me to report to Room 203 after my physical.

I proceeded through the whole examination and was finally brought to see the psychiatrist. I had let my blond hair grow out deliberately, hoping that they would ask if I bleached it, but no one did. During the course of his questioning, he noted that I had been arrested.

"What were you arrested for?" he asked.

"Dressing like a woman," I replied.

With that he excused himself and left the room, only to return with another man, who I learned was the chief psychiatrist. He asked, "Tell me, when you go in women's clothes, do you wear a hat?"

Fluttering my eyelashes at him, I replied, "Good gracious, no, it'll look as if I were covering something. I just let my hair grow long and curl it."

Both men turned to look at one another. Then one asked, "You mention that you're both active and passive. Tell me, do you like to stick your dick up some shitty ass-hole?"

I batted my eyelashes even faster and looked directly at him and said, "Yes. You should try it some time, it isn't half bad, you know!"

With that answer they both left the room. When they did, I took out some very strong perfume I had taken with me and poured it all over myself. A few minutes later, one of the men came in and told me I could go and finish the examination.

After it was completed, I got on a long, single line as a man at a large desk stamped each application "Accepted" or "Rejected." Those who were accepted were to report to the doctor for injections. As I stood there, it occurred to me that I hadn't filled out a homosexual questionnaire, as I knew others had done who had taken their physicals long before me. *They're gonna take me,* I thought. *I'll pass out, I know it; I'll faint right on the spot if they take me.*

As I approached the desk, the man behind it was smiling and reached for my application. Suddenly his smile disappeared, and he reached over the length of the desk to pick up a stamp and stamped the paper with all his strength, and then just about threw it at me. It fell from the desk to the floor, and he said, "Okay, honey, you made it; you're out."

I picked up the paper, smiled back at him, and said, "Thank you." As I did so, the man behind me must have picked up on what was going on because he gave me a slight push, which almost threw me off balance. I turned, gave him a dirty look, and said to the man behind the desk, "Aren't I supposed to report to Room 203?"

"No, it's not necessary now."

I thanked him again and left the building.

I expected that Bill would be along soon and decided to wait for him. He was to report after me, and I had been in there three hours, so I figured I'd wait just a little while. As I stood on the steps of Whitehall Street, a bus loaded with recruits for the army was parked across the street. Some of the men began calling to me. "Hey, honey, I got a big one for you. Nine inches."

"Mine's ten," shouted another.

I didn't want any trouble and decided the best thing to do was to get as far away from there as possible. I walked a few blocks and went into a restaurant and decided to try Bill, thinking that perhaps he may not have gone. I was surprised when he answered.

"Didn't you go for your physical?" I asked.

"Yes, I was there for about twenty minutes," he answered.

"Twenty minutes!" I repeated. "How could you be there for such a short time? I was there almost three hours."

"Baby, I went there flaming. I wore a black turtleneck, makeup for days, and a ladies' pin, and told them I was gay. They said they didn't want me and let me go."

We spoke for a few more minutes, and then I told him I would see him the following week at the party we were having and hung up.

Imagine that: twenty minutes. I wouldn't have had that much nerve. I smiled to myself as I took the train home to the Bronx.

I told my parents the reason I wasn't accepted was due to a heart murmur. I told them there was nothing to worry about, but the army felt it best I stay out. They seemed to accept it, and the issue was fortunately dropped.

Alan, full of wild ideas, had thought it would be a camp to have a mock wedding since Terry had purchased a wedding gown a few weeks before. He had bought the gown for its material value since it was so reasonable. He had intended to use the material to make something for his sister. He sewed beautifully and often made his own clothes. Alan wanted to be the bride with Pat, Harold, and me as his attendants. Ed, a next-door neighbor of Johnny's consented to act as groom; since it was all in jest. So, Terry began his sewing on, of all things, crepe paper. The only material gown would be the bride's.

The wedding night arrived, and the guests assembled in Johnny's apartment. He was to act as minister, although Ernest volunteered his services. Bill was there, and so was Joe and several others. Terry, in the meantime, had taken a room upstairs above Johnny's apartment, which had become vacant, and we were to dress there. We soon discovered that Ed, the groom, could not attend because he had a date that he had forgotten about. "Very convenient," said Alan. "*Now* what do we do?" Since Joe was the only guest attired in a black suit and tie, he was elected, much to his dismay. However, he decided to go through with it.

As the phonograph played the *Wedding March*, we left the upstairs apartment and slowly walked down the stairs to Johnny's apartment. Since I was the shortest, I led, wearing my powder blue gown, followed by Pat in an identical dress of very light yellow. Then came Harold dressed in another style of light green, followed by Alan and Joe.

The gowns were really lovely, and if they had been made of real material, could have easily been sold in a store. Terry had done a terrific job on them, both in designing and sewing them; a difficult task, considering they were made out of paper. When the ceremony was over, I rushed upstairs with Bill to change my outfit. I had borrowed a red evening gown and wanted to wear that. After changing, we went downstairs and joined the party. We danced and enjoyed ourselves until the liquor ran out and people started leaving. As Joe was leaving, we all thanked him for being such a good sport about everything. "Oh, I didn't mind, really. It was fun!" he said and left.

With the warm weather once again upon us, we started going to the beach, and then thoughts went to vacation time.

My second trip to the Cape was again with Terry, Johnny,

Nicky, Pat, and a friend of Pat's named Billy (who was also a fashion designer, as we will see later). The three of us took a cabin across the street from the post office, and Pat and Billy took a double room in the building next door to the cabins, which was owned by the same people.

The Cape held pleasant and unpleasant memories for me of the year before with Bill. However, since I was now alone, I intended to make the most of it, and I did, meeting a number of people. I also had my long hair cut to a crew-cut, which was becoming very popular. My hair was now platinum blonde and the barber said, "Girls would die to have hair this color." I said nothing but thought, *They can just get Clairol!*

A week later, our vacation was over. How fast time goes when you're having fun. We took the boat back to Boston, as we had done the first time, then the bus to New York and back to the grind of everyday work.

The weeks and months went by so quickly that before long it was Christmas, and for New Year's Eve 1951–52 we did the Times Square number. I hated it and swore I'd never go there again.

We attended a party a few weeks later at the apartment of two friends of Joe's named George and Bobby, whom I found to be very nice and friendly. I asked a friend of mine, Chuck Douglas, to come with me. Chuck and I lived in the same neighborhood, and we had seen each other many mornings getting off the train on our way home from the bars. We became friendly; nothing sexual. I liked Chuck. He was full of fun, and we got along very well.

Another party was on the agenda for my birthday in June. This time it was held in New Jersey at the home of still another friend from the bars, by the name of Manny. He had recently joined the navy and was home on leave. He also had a friend whose birthday was the same day as mine, so we decided it would be nice to have a joint celebration. We took pictures and had a wonderful time. I took one picture with Manny, and he liked it so much when he saw it that he kept it in his wallet.

From constant patronizing of one particular bar I liked, and also due to the fact that we worked in the same building, I became very friendly with George Jennings and Jerry Leighman. George was of Polish extraction, about five feet eight inches tall with dark brown hair and blue eyes and was around 140 pounds. He resembled the movie actor Jackie Cooper. Jerry was Jewish and about the same height as George but much thinner with dark brown wavy hair and brown eyes. We went everywhere together; but mostly I went with George because Jerry was a bit of a loner. Many people thought George and I were lovers, and we did everything to prove we were nothing more than "sisters."

With the warm weather once again, we decided to go to the Cape. I loved the place at this point, and since George and Jerry hadn't been there, it would be fun showing them around. We planned our vacation for the first two weeks of July, as I had been doing now for almost two years.

George and I wanted to have our hair bleached and asked Joe's friend Bobby to do it for us. He agreed, and it took me one hour to become a platinum blond. George took two applications since his hair was darker than mine originally.

Thinking we were a sensation, the three of us left by bus for Boston. When we arrived, we discovered that the last bus for P Town had already left, as had the boat. Jerry suggested we fly. I had never flown and was very nervous about the mere suggestion. Nonetheless, I agreed.

The plane was very small: only ten seats, five on each side. I sat on the left-hand side of the two-engine plane with George in front of me and Jerry to my right. After I strapped myself in, I looked in the pocket of the seat in front of me and picked up a magazine. I was really nervous as the plane slowly taxied down the runway. Presently we stopped, then the engines began to spin faster, and the plane started down the runway. My heart was in my mouth as the tiny plane lifted from the ground, and we were airborne.

I was looking out the window when I felt Jerry's hand tap me. I turned and he asked how I felt.

"This is great! I should have done this years ago."

We were no sooner in the air than it seemed we had landed at the Provincetown airport. Such a short ride: only twenty minutes. I was not disappointed because I had enjoyed the ride. We got into a taxi and proceeded to the rooming house where we had reservations.

During the week, I again had my hair cut into a crew cut and decided that the color was too light. After being in the sun a few days it had lightened tremendously. I darkened it and felt it looked much better. Again, before we realized it, the vacation was over, and we returned to New York via plane to Boston and bus back to the city.

With Thanksgiving again approaching, I asked Terry to make my outfit for the drag. The gown he made for me was a copy of one I had seen on a TV show. It was strapless, done in turquoise, with a white brocade bolero jacket. On the hips were two large bows with streamers of the same material as the jacket. It was slit in the front about twelve inches to give me room to walk, but it was still so tight that I could hardly move my legs up one step. I had my short hair done at a friend's beauty salon, dressed in another friend's apartment on the West Side, and then went off to the dance with Joe and Terry. It was jammed, as usual, and we took pictures, but I still refused to enter the Grand March, although everyone said I looked sensational. I knew I looked good, but in the first place, I couldn't possibly have gotten up the steps leading to the stage, and, secondly, I was too frightened. At the end of the evening, we took a cab to the apartment I had dressed in, changed, and returned home. Again, the next day was a workday.

New Year's Eve of 1952–53 was spent at George and Bobby's apartment, where champagne was plentiful. We were so tired at the end of the evening after most of the guests had left, that I and a few others fell asleep on the couch. Next morning we were served champagne with peaches, which was delicious, and then I made my way home.

EIGHT

In February, George gave a party for his birthday at the apartment of a friend of his. I decided once again to go in drag, and taking the turquoise gown, made some changes. I added, in place of the bolero jacket, white tulle, cut the dress at the knees, and added more white tulle. The jokes had begun about my dress. "She's started," said one guest. "I've noticed," replied another, but I knew they were said in good humor, so it didn't bother me.

George, Jerry, and I once again decided to go to the Cape for vacation and selected the same time of year as we had the year before. We followed the same procedure as the previous year, bus and plane. The only time the three of us were together was at the beach and for dinner. Some nights Jerry would have a date, or George, or I. We all had our own type and were meeting new people. The weather was perfect, and George and Jerry developed beautiful tans. I envied them since I didn't tan, but just got red and peeled. However, after a few days there, I did start to develop a slight tan, and I felt wonderful. I was careful to select clothes that would enhance it: whites, pastel colors, especially light blue—my favorite color!

One afternoon I returned from the beach early, as I usually did because I couldn't take too much sun. After I had showered, shaved, and changed clothes, I decided to go to the bar for a few drinks and see the show, which I had heard was very good. I had met an older man during the week and ran into him when I arrived at the bar. we talked for awhile, the show started. It was good and extremely funny. During the course of it, George and Jerry arrived and joined our table. While laughing at the jokes of one of the comedians, the audience would glance at one another and smile. As I was doing this, my eyes fell on a very handsome man with dark hair and glasses seated at a nearby table. His eyes also rested on mine, and we held the stare for a few minutes before returning our attention to the entertainer. During the remainder of the show, I glanced from time to time at this man, hoping his eyes would be there to meet mine. They were, and I was delighted!

When the show was over, we began talking. His name was Connie Lucia. He asked me to have dinner with him, and I gladly accepted. We arranged a time and place to meet, and then he left the bar. A few minutes later, I decided to leave as well. The man I was with asked me where I was going. "Home to change and then to dinner," I replied.

"I thought we were having dinner together tonight?" he replied.

"We were, but we're not now; I've changed my mind. Good night," and with that we left the bar. I was surprised at myself for being so rude, but *What the hell,* I thought, *Connie's much nicer, anyway!*

We met for dinner as planned and had an enjoyable evening. We saw the show at the cocktail bar, then went to another bar to see its show. I liked Connie and felt very good being with him. At twelve o'clock the bars closed, and there was no place else to go. I suggested we go to my place, and he agreed. I didn't realize how attractive he was until he took off his glasses, but it didn't matter. We liked each other, and we were alone together; that's all that mattered.

After our return from the Cape, Connie and I saw each other often. We would go to movies or plays, then for a drink at a nightclub. I enjoyed his company very much, but I did wish we had an apartment to which to go or stay home a bit more.

Just seeing him and being together would have to do. He took me to see *New Faces of '52,* and this was the first time I saw Eartha Kitt, whose singing I really enjoyed.

There was a strangeness about him that I couldn't understand, and I questioned him about it often but did not receive a satisfactory answer, so I let the matter drop. One night he said, "I can't explain it, Tom. I'm funny. It's got nothing to do with you; it's me. You'll just have to put up with my crazy carrying-on."

"Connie, I'm not even going to try to understand you. I just hope we'll be good friends as we are tonight. I think you're the greatest. You're good to me, always insist on paying; it's all very nice, but I wish once in awhile you'd let me pay for something."

"So, who's complaining? Do you ever hear me complain about paying?"

"No, but, well—"

"No buts, just enjoy it. If you don't, someone else will."

I got the message loud and clear and dropped the subject. It was getting late, and he had to catch his train, so we each said good night.

We didn't see too much of each other in the weeks that followed but did keep in touch by phone. Occasionally we'd meet for lunch, and I would invite him to any party that happened along. Whenever I did, he always showed up with a bottle of liquor. It annoyed me, and I told him it wasn't necessary.

"I don't mind, Tom. I hate to come without something," he would tell me. It got to a point where I didn't bother to mention it again. *Still* he brought a bottle!

Labor Day we went to Fire Island, to which I had never been. The beach was beautiful and we had a very good time. Although I liked it, I still wasn't that terribly impressed after having heard so much about it from different people.

Atlantic City (AC) held a Halloween drag, and with Terry and George I attended. Out came the turquoise gown, this time the trimmings were changed from white to black. I decided it wouldn't be too bad since no one had seen it in Atlantic City. The poor dress was beginning to see its day.

Another drag in New Jersey came up shortly after we returned from AC, and once more out came the turquoise to be changed once again. This time I replaced the black tulle top with a black jacket, removed the tulle bottom, cut the dress to just below the hips, and added a full, black jersey bottom. When Terry saw it, he laughed and said he couldn't believe it. "What other plans do you have for it?" he asked. When Joe saw the pictures of still another change, he suggested it might look well as a bra or hankie. I told him I'd give the matter serious consideration.

We dressed at the apartment of Joe's sister, Helenmae, who lived in New Jersey in a town close to where the drag was being held. George and Terry also went in drag, George in a striped bathing suit with a large red rose on the top in the center of the bosom, and Terry as a flapper. Terry and I had hit every thrift shop on Third Avenue a few weeks before, looking for an appropriate pair of shoes in keeping with his outfit, until we finally found them. He won a prize for one of the most original costumes. Later we went to another bar, and during the course of the evening George and I went to the men's room. As George was leaning over to flush the toilet, the rose in his bosom fell into the toilet and was flushed. The towels in the bathing suit that served to make his hips larger kept slipping, and from time to time we had to stuff them back up. Such a mess, but fun!

In November I attended the ball with Chuck Douglas. For this Terry had made me a light green tight-fitting tailored suit. My hair was long and light blond again, so George, who by this time had completed his hairdressing training, put a red rinse in it, set, and combed it out. It looked beautiful. Again, before the twelve-o'clock deadline we were on our way home to avoid any trouble, although with Chuck I wasn't afraid since he was well over six feet tall and built on the muscular side. After changing, he and I took the train back to the Bronx.

Christmas was not far off, and I began buying gifts for my family and friends. On Christmas Eve, Joe invited me to a small party after we attended church services. I asked him if it would be all right to invite Connie, and he said of course.

The party was at the house of one of Joe's friends named Eric Johns. After introductions were made, we also met a striking woman by the name of Marie O'Toole. Marie and Eric had known each other for many years. Joe had met Eric one evening, and after several dates they became friendly. Joe and Marie had also become good friends and went everywhere together. She was about six feet and resembled the movie actress Jane Russell. In fact, she had won a look-alike contest and had done publicity work for one of Miss Russell's recent movies. She did modeling as well.

I liked them immediately! They seemed sincere and very down-to-earth. After Connie arrived, we all attended church services, then returned to Eric's and listened to Christmas carols, had a few drinks, and exchanged gifts. Everyone liked Connie. What was there not to like about him? His easygoing nature made it impossible for anyone not to like him, and it felt good being with him again.

He surprised me when he handed me a small, gift-wrapped package. "Nothing much," he said, "just wanted to give you something!" It was a beautiful pair of cuff links and tie clasp to match in silver with a small diamond in the center.

"They're beautiful, Connie, thank you very much."

We all sat around listening to more music for some time. It was so quiet, you could hear a pin drop. Soon the night had become early morning, and it was time to leave. Connie and I took a cab to Grand Central Terminal, said our farewells, and left.

The week that followed was spent in deciding what party

invitation to accept for New Year's Eve. Everyone had some place to go, and yet we all wanted to be together. Since no one had an apartment large enough to give a party, we all began accepting invitations.

Early in the afternoon of New Year's Eve, I received a phone call from a Puerto Rican boy I had met recently in a bar. His name was Andy Santiago. Although Puerto Rican, he had natural light blond hair and greenish-brown eyes. He was slightly shorter than me, and we had not had an affair as yet. We were both interested but somehow hadn't gotten around to it. He asked me, "What are you doing tonight, Tommy?"

"Going to a party downtown," I answered. "And you?"

"I have no plans, that's why I'm calling you."

"Gee, I wish I could invite you, but, to tell the truth, I'm going on someone else's invitation."

"Well, Tommy, why don't you and your friends come over here, and we can have a little party of our own? My place is large, and it would be so much fun being with you."

"That sounds great, Andy. Let me make a few calls, and I'll call you back. Give me the address so that if we decide to come everyone will have it."

He gave me the address, and I made several calls. To my surprise, almost everyone I called said they would rather be together than go to where they were going.

About an hour later, I called Andy back. "Okay, kid, you've got yourself a party. I'll be over around eight to help you."

"Wonderful, Tommy. Err . . . how many people did you invite?"

"Not too many, about fifteen or twenty," I told him.

"That sounds great. See you later."

Fifteen or twenty, I said to myself after I hung up the phone, *if he only knew it would be more like fifty.*

And so New Year's Eve of 1953–54 was spent at Andy's. By midnight the fifteen or twenty people I had invited turned out to be more in the eighty or ninety bracket. Everyone, it seemed, brought a friend, and there were people none of us knew. Everyone brought a bottle of liquor, and everything ran smoothly. Considering the amount of people, there were no drunks, no fights, no one spilling anything, and all seemed to be enjoying themselves.

When the last guest had left, we discovered there was plenty of liquor left over and decided that the following Sunday afternoon we would have some people over again. Andy was beginning to like the idea of another party and couldn't wait for Sunday to come.

Sunday came and about twenty or twenty-five people showed up. Again, things seemed to be going along well—plenty of liquor for everyone. In fact, some of the guests had brought more liquor with them.

During the course of the evening, I was sitting on the couch talking with a friend while Andy was in the kitchen fixing drinks, when we heard a scream coming from the bedroom. We ran in to find one of the guests with his pants off and dancing on top of the bed. "What the hell is this?" I asked in anger. "What do you think you're doing?"

"Oh, joost a widdle dance for the boys," said the stranger. "Ya mind?"

"I certainly do. Andy is nice enough to have us over, and you have to pull something like this. If you want to stay, you'd better put your pants on."

"Killjoy!" said another guest.

"And that goes for you!" I snapped back. "And if you don't like it, you can leave with him. You won't be missed."

When I returned to the living room, the other guests asked what had happened, and I told them. They laughed and said the kid was just drunk, and I shouldn't take things so seriously.

"I'm not taking anything seriously. If they want to carry on, fine, but they can do it in their own apartments. Andy was nice enough to let us have a party; why should we ruin it for ourselves?"

"I suppose you're right, Tom," said another guest.

Andy joined the group, and I told him how sorry I was about the whole matter. He told me to forget it since no harm had been done, then he asked me to dance.

I was annoyed most of the evening after that. I had never seen anything like that before. Sure, I had heard of gang bangs, which I have never been to but would discover later in life, but this was different. I was beginning to learn that there was much to come and different types of people I would meet before long.

Several weeks later Andy called and told me he was going into the navy. I tried to talk him out of it and suggested he wait until he was drafted since it would be only two years rather than four in the navy. He told me he wanted to get it over with, and that he always wanted to travel, so what better way than in the navy?

The night before he was to leave, Andy, several others, and I had dinner in a restaurant. Andy was nervous and felt sad at leaving, and everyone at the table sensed this and tried to cheer him up. We told of hearing stories about sailors in various predicaments and joked for hours. As we left the restaurant, I said to him, "Andy, please write to me. Don't be like all the others who say they will and never do."

"I won't, Tommy. You're like a brother to me, and I hope our friendship never ends."

"I hope so too, Andy."

With that we said good-bye, and he was gone. We had become such good friends that the thought of sex didn't enter into it, although I did sleep with him one night, and we sort of fooled around but nothing serious. Besides, he was too huge!

Andy was true to his promise to write often, and I answered just as soon as I heard from him.

NINE

The following February, George and Joe decided to have a joint birthday party. Their birthdays were just days apart. Joe's friends George and Bobby had broken up, and Bobby was living alone, so they held the party in his apartment. The apartment was jammed. I had invited some "straight" boys from work and also a straight girl I worked with. Naturally, I invited Connie. Marie was there, Bill, Joe's sister, Helenmae, Eric—everyone. We now had our own clique. We called it "us," and whenever "us" gave a party, rest assured if only "us" came and no one else, the apartment would be jammed. Connie and Marie got along very well together. We took pictures, as usual, and in general had one hell of a time.

I had been corresponding for some time with a boy named Gerry who was in the navy with Manny. He had seen the picture Manny and I had taken together at my birthday party at Manny's apartment some time before and asked Manny if I would write him. He sent me his picture, and I almost flipped when I saw it. He was beautiful! Light blond hair, blue eyes, nice build, and his letters were so interesting. True, he wasn't what I would normally call "my type" by any stretch of the Imagination, but he was extremely attractive. A letter arrived one afternoon telling me that he would be in New York on May 2 and asked me to meet him at the airport.

We seemed to have missed each other after his flight arrived, so I had him paged. As he came through the door, I recognized him immediately. We exchanged greetings and took a cab to Manhattan to the apartment of a friend of mine who was out of town. I had the keys and had planned to spend some time with Gerry at the apartment. When we arrived there, I sensed something was wrong but couldn't figure out what. He told me later that I wasn't his type, and he was sorry. I felt a bit hurt, but what could I do? Here I had everything planned, and what was happening—nothing. *Oh, well,* I thought, *here I go again!* Type or no type, we did have a sexual one-nighter.

Gerry remained in New York for a few weeks and then returned to his native Chicago since he was now out of the service. We continued from time to time to correspond, but eventually that faded. So many things were fading lately. Time was really going fast.

I always wanted to have a surprise birthday party, so I decided to have one. I planned everything with the help of Joe and Helenmae. The party was to be held at Eric's the day after my birthday. When I arrived, I was supposed to act surprised. After my arrival and bit of "acting," I went over to Helenmae and asked her how I did.

"You'll never win an Oscar, honey." She smiled.

"I agree, but I felt so silly."

"You are silly," echoed Joe, smiling.

It was a very warm evening, and since the apartment didn't have air-conditioning, I changed into a light blue bathing suit, and we took pictures. When we saw them later, it looked as though I didn't have any clothes on at all. How embarrassing!

After a few months of more warm weather and going to the beach, the fall once again was upon us. Joe, George, and I decided we would go to Atlantic City for the drag. Joe now had an apartment of his own on West Twenty-second Street, which George shared with him, although he still lived at home with his parents.

Halloween night found us in AC. Stan, a friend we had met recently and who was also a hairdresser, decided to join us. He was going in drag, too, for the first time. From Joe I borrowed a black velvet A-line, street-length dress and bought a pair of black high heels. My hair was very light blond, and Stan put a blue rinse in it, set it with double waves on each side, and waved the back. When he was finished, he said, "Okay, honey, you're finished—out so we can get ready."

I took a walk with two boys who came with us, one of whom was to be my escort. We walked in the cool evening for a while then decided to go back to the hotel to see if the others were ready. They weren't, so to kill some time we went to the bar below the hotel. We were in there for a short time when an argument in the back broke out. "You fuckin' dizzy queen, I ought to kill you," said one man to another in a very loud voice. The bar was not crowded, and we just sat there looking at the fight and drinking our drinks.

Later when we left and joined the others, they asked what was going on. After I told them, Joe said, "Oh, we thought someone was killing you."

I smiled and said, "No, dear, they didn't pick up on me at all, so there!"

We went on to the dance and another enjoyable evening.

Thanksgiving again found me at the ball. This time I borrowed a powder blue silk dress from a friend of Joe's and had Stan do my hair and escort me. I ran into Bill Lopez, who said I looked beautiful and was beginning to show "promise," whatever that meant. We took pictures and ran into many friends. As usual, I left before the midnight deadline because there was work the following day.

On Christmas Eve after dinner, we went to a dance in New Jersey. There I met a very nice Italian boy by the name of Johnny Tyler. We danced for some time and at the end of the evening exchanged phone numbers. I asked him to Stan's New Year's Eve party, and he said he would love to come. We spoke during the week, and I gave him the address.

So, New Year's Eve of 1954–55 was spent at Stan's East Side apartment. It was a very large duplex, complete with staircase and piano: a drag queen's delight! Imagine coming down the staircase, as I had done at a previous party in a black beaded sheath with black chiffon across the bosom, flowing to the floor, and sitting on top of the piano. Sheer heaven!

At the party, we were wondering what had happened to George, or, as he was also known, Jennie. It was getting late, and he hadn't arrived yet. About a half hour later, he arrived in full drag. He had on a silver street-length dress and a large furry-type hat. I noticed that his arm was held against his chest and assumed that it was just a camp position. After his entrance, he asked a friend to take him to the hospital. He had dislocated his shoulder when he fell down the steps of the stoop and landed against a car. We ripped his dress off because he couldn't get it over his head and took off as much of the makeup as we could. Then he went to the hospital.

About two hours later he returned with his arm in a sling. "What a hell of a way to start the New Year," he said on entering the apartment.

"As long as you're okay, that's the important thing," remarked another guest.

Johnny and I spent the night at Stan's, and somehow we didn't get along sexually. We decided that we would be better off being friends than trying for a love affair. In the morning we said good-bye, and he promised to call, which he did the following evening, and we saw each other almost every weekend. We went to the bars or to a movie, but never again slept together. We had become good friends. A few weeks later, Johnny met someone and before long was seeing him on a steady basis. They eventually became lovers and shared an apartment.

It was now March of 1955, and for months I hadn't been feeling well. Each night I would come home from work and go right to bed. I had no desire for food. In fact, the thought of it upset me very much. Toward the end of the month, I told Joe what was wrong, and he said his brother-in-law had been sent to the hospital with yellow jaundice, and that it sounded as if I had the same thing.

"I don't want to frighten you, Tom, but you'd better see a doctor to be on the safe side."

I was frightened at the thought that I, too, might have it, but I also wanted to be sure, so I went to the doctor. Sure enough, I had it, and he made arrangements for me to enter the hospital. I had never been in a hospital as a patient, only to visit others, and I was naturally upset not knowing what the treatment for this disease would be. I soon learned! Injections in my rear every morning, pills of various sizes and colors, intravenous feeding the first night, no fatty foods, but, worst of all, no liquor. I was pissed, too, because I had made arrangements to have a party at a friend's house on Riverside Drive for the following Saturday. When my friends came on Sunday, they said the party had been a huge success, which pissed me off even more, but I smiled through it. I was only supposed to have two people at a time around my bed, but there were times I had eight. The nurses were so sweet they didn't ask anyone to leave.

After my release from the hospital nine days later, I remained home for another two weeks and then returned to work. My weight had dropped seven pounds, and I had no desire to smoke until one day I decided to try again. Gradually, I began smoking again, much to my regret!

Whenever George and I would go out on weekends, I would order Cokes or sodas, not mixed, and since I had to pay for the liquor, anyway, gave it to him. At times when we left the bars, he was quite high.

Terry called one evening to tell me he was tired of New York and was moving to California. I felt bad at the thought of losing such a good friend. We promised to keep in touch, and whenever he wrote, I answered almost immediately. I hadn't seen Harold, Pat, or Alan for some time. We all had our own interests now, and only occasionally would we get together for a movie or meet for drinks.

I started bartender's school at night with a boy I had recently met named Kim. Six weeks later we finished the course. The school promised to place us, but after graduation little came of it.

For the Fourth of July, Stan and I went to Atlantic City again. I was still drinking Cokes or sodas. One afternoon we returned from the beach, changed, and showered. From Stan I borrowed a black short-sleeved waist shirt, cut low in a V shape in the center, and had a side zipper. I wore a skintight, boxer-type orange bathing suit, white sandals, and around my neck a small cultured pearl, which George and Stan had given me the previous Christmas. My hair was platinum blonde.

When Stan and I arrived at the bar, it was already crowded. As I entered, the people moved to the sides to get a better look at what I was wearing. I felt marvelous, and with the bit of color I had gotten from the beach, I knew I looked good. We went to the bar, ordered drinks, and returned to the center of the room. We were there a short while, standing next to several people. One of the boys was in the midst of camping and making everyone around laugh. He had light blond hair, blue eyes, was taller than me, and about the same age. He had a nice tan and was wearing a pullover shirt with a huge pocket in the center about the waist. He started singing along with the jukebox and changing some of the words to his own and had everyone in hysterics. We all laughed, and he introduced himself. His name was Bill Bushe. We were soon all camping together, and, before long, people started throwing money on the floor near us, which we picked up.

"I'm too lazy to go home and get more money," he said, "and I'm only staying a few houses from here."

"Me, too," I said, "and we're only across the street."

We laughed and continued this for some time and collected enough money for several more drinks. When cocktail time was over, we arranged to meet later for dinner, and the three of us were together for the remainder of the weekend.

We took the bus home and exchanged phone numbers. I liked Bill—not sexually, but it was refreshing to meet someone so lively and funny, and, let's face it, who doesn't like to laugh? We called each other after our return, and he started joining us on weekends.

Seven months after my hepatitis attack, I started drinking beer. My weight increased five pounds and stayed at that for some time.

Joe had been working for a department store that had long since closed and had taken furs and dresses and whatever else he thought we might need. He had taken so many things, we needed a closet just for our drags. Came in handy when we wanted to outdo other drags, as they were very fashionable.

On Thanksgiving, I borrowed a black, two-piece velvet suit from Joe and after dinner had my hair done at a beauty salon that was closed to the public but open only for the gay guys. Along with the suit I wore a plain white blouse and furs over my shoulders. A face veil completed the outfit.

When I arrived at the dance, I walked to the box office and purchased my ticket. I looked good and knew it! As I entered, I ran into George, who couldn't get over how well I looked and kept complimenting me on the outfit. It made me feel very good because I had come to depend on both Joe and George for their opinions as to what to wear and what I would look best in. If their opinions were against mine, I would usually follow their advice.

When the dance was over, Joe and I took the subway to the Bronx. He took me to my house, and I was in my bedroom taking off my outfit in the dark when my mother came out of her bedroom to use the bathroom. I quickly ducked into the closet so she couldn't see me. Since it was dark, all she could see was something black bent over. She said hello to Joe, went to the bathroom, and then returned to her room. I sighed a sigh of relief. *Thank goodness she didn't see me,* I thought. *What nerve I have coming home like this in full drag!*

Christmas and New Year's came, and we spent New Year's Eve of 1955–56 in a bar that was a bit different from our usual routine and dull. In February I started working part-time on Saturday and Sunday in a gay bar as a bartender. I did this just for the experience and received no salary. I did, however, receive tips, such as they were because the bar was never that crowded.

Being platinum blonde behind the bar, I was known as Jean Harlow. Joe would come with me when I opened at three o'clock and sit at the very end of the bar. I took the largest glass in the place and filled it with rum and the slightest bit of Coke. "Twenty-five cents, please," I would ask him. As the afternoon wore on and he had finished his drink, I would refill it the same way, and most of the time didn't charge him other than the initial time for his drinks.

One afternoon, as I was waiting on customers, two young men came in and ordered drinks. One of them had very light blond hair cut in a crew, blue eyes, and was about five feet eleven inches tall. When I gave him his change, he held my hand and asked my name. I told him. He said his name was Roger Powers. He came from Washington, D.C., and was in New York on business. He asked me to join him when I had finished work, and since Joe had already left, I joined him.

Roger seemed very nice and was rather attractive. His friend left, and we continued talking for some time. We then had dinner and went to a movie. When we left the movie, the snow that had started earlier really had piled up and was very deep. We took a cab to Joe's apartment and made love. I enjoyed sex with him very much, and since he had to be up early the next day for a meeting, he gave me his address and said he would write. A few weeks later, I received a letter from him. He was coming to town again on business and wanted to get together.

The evening after he arrived, we went to a party. There was a number of people there, and there was a show in progress as we arrived, and we were asked to contribute fifty cents for admission. I don't recall what it was for, but we didn't argue. Joe and several others were also there. Marie and Eric hadn't arrived yet but were expected.

A few hours later, the police arrived and said they had a complaint that there was too much noise, and, before we realized what was happening, we were put under arrest for disturbing the peace. All the women at the party were allowed to leave with escorts, so Eric and Marie left together.

Into the police wagon we went. "Here I go again," I said to Joe. "Only this time in my own clothes."

"That's a switch, isn't it," he replied.

It turned out there were eighty-two of us, and it made the papers the next day. We were scattered all over town. I managed to stay with Joe and Roger, and I felt terrible about bringing Roger to a party and having it raided, but he seemed to be enjoying it. "Don't worry about it. What can they do but fine us for disorderly conduct?" he mused.

After we had been booked, the sergeant at the desk looked up and asked if anyone could type because he was getting tired. Had he looked at my "rap sheet," I think they call it, he would have seen that I was a typist, but I'd be damned if I was going to help them.

We were put in separate cells, and in the morning one of the policemen asked if we would like some coffee. I was running out of cigarettes and asked if he would get me some, which he did. Wrong brand, but why complain?

We were taken downtown and fined ten dollars for disorderly conduct. One poor guy didn't have any money, so some of us chipped in and bailed him out. *Well,* I thought, *this makes two for Miss D.* The next day we laughed about it, and Roger returned to Washington, but not before we had another session in bed.

Joe and I had planned on attending the Bal Fantastique, so we rented a suite of rooms at the Astor Hotel, where it was being held. We didn't want to have to go into the street and thought it would be much easier for us to go directly from our rooms by elevator and into the ballroom. The night of the ball, Joe and I checked into the room and started preparing ourselves. George and Stan came to help with the hair and anything we might need. I wore a powder blue sequin bathing suit with a large blue overskirt. George did my hair pushed back off the face with an attachment in back forming a ponytail. Joe was to wear a black bathing suit and a Norwegian fox stole.

As Joe was dressing, something wasn't right, and he decided not to go. I was wrecked! I didn't want to go by myself. George said he would go in Joe's place and would wear his outfit. He started preparing himself, when he discovered he didn't have shoes. Stan offered to lend him a pair he had and went home to get them. Johnny Tyler went dressed as a pirate with a false moustache and looked great.

When we left the room, we discovered the elevator did not go to the ballroom. We had to get off at the lobby, go into the street, and walk around the corner to the ballroom entrance. The street was crowded with spectators watching the arrival of the costumed people. We had secured our tickets from Marie, and the stipulation of the discounted tickets was that the holders must wear costumes or evening wear.

When we finally entered the ballroom, it was jammed with people in various costumes and evening clothes. We walked around for some time, had several drinks, and at one point as we were passing a large table filled with people, they started talking with us and asked me to pose for pictures with them—on top of the table, yet! I did, and later as we passed another table, which was empty, the occupants apparently dancing, we saw a bottle of scotch, and with one scoop over the table, the bottle was gone and under my skirt. We took it to our room after the dance and finished it.

Like years before, when October came my thoughts again centered on what to wear for the annual drag. I had changed my mind several times already, and then one day at work some stills came in of a new movie that would be released soon. I liked one of the gowns and asked a friend to make it. I thought if my timing were right, I could wear it before the picture was released, thereby making it seem like an original.

I had Billy, Pat's friend who was with us in P Town a few years before, make it for me. Of course, I had to pay him. Terry never took money for any work he did for me. After several fittings and three weeks of work, the gown was ready. It was a strapless sheath of white brocade, with scattered white flowers on a three-leaf stem. Across the bosom was powder blue taffeta, coming around to the back, meeting, and forming a bow with two large streamers just touching the floor. Into each of the little flowers I placed tiny rhinestones. The sides of the gown had inverted pleats so that I had ample room to walk, and not hobble as I did with the first gown I had worn. From Joe I borrowed the beautiful three-tier Norwegian fox stole. George set my hair, and Stan combed it out. It was done bouffant style, with curls on the forehead. I dressed at the apartment of a friend on the Lower East Side.

Johnny Tyler agreed to escort me, and Phil Kent and Bob Conway, whom I'd met through Bill Lopez and who were also lovers, came over to see me, as did Willie, a boy who had been coming to my office for pictures of movie stars. Again we took pictures, and I knew I looked sensational. We drove most of the way in Johnny's car, parked it a few blocks from the dance, and transferred to Bob's car. He wasn't going to attend, but said he would pick us up just before the dance ended.

When we arrived, as usual, the outside of the ballroom was jammed with people. It was like a Hollywood premiere, people shouting and screaming as we entered. I posed for pictures and felt like a movie star. When the final picture was taken, I turned, and we entered the ballroom. Again, there was the double line of people inside the ballroom, and several people called to me; I smiled and nodded my greeting. I felt wonderful. Never in the past years had so much attention been given to me. It was marvelous!

When the Grand March was announced, I decided for the first time to enter. After much shoving and pushing by the other contestants, I managed to get to the stage and walked across it slowly, making sure that everyone got a good look at the gown. There was applause, and it made me feel very good.

When I came down, George and Stan had arrived. They had gone to dinner earlier and had not seen me completely dressed. They were extremely pleased at how I looked and told me so. We made arrangements to return to the apartment, where I dressed and took the rest of the pictures, and, after excusing myself, Johnny and I went to the bar for a drink.

Stan didn't show up at the apartment, and I assumed he was with George. About an hour later, after the pictures were taken, the phone rang. It was George! "I'm over at the bar and half the dance is here. Come on over," he said.

I told him I couldn't because I had changed already.

"Well, you're missing a good time. If you change your mind, come over. If not, I'll call you tomorrow."

I told him I doubted I would come, and we hung up. I told the others about it, and for a few minutes there was the thought I might get dressed again and go, but I finally decided against it. "You people can go if you want to," I said, "but tomorrow's work, and I'm beat!"

The next day George phoned and asked if Stan had been with me the night before. I told him no, that I thought he was with him. *What a mix-up, I thought. He must be furious with us.* Furious wasn't the word! When I called him to explain that I thought George was with him and George thought he was with me, he said it was all right but was very cool to us after that and didn't call either of us very often. Seems he got lost in the crowd and didn't know the exact address or phone number of where I had dressed because he had come with George originally. I felt bad for some time because I really liked Stan.

A week or so later I was in a bar in the Village with Johnny, when a dark-haired boy came in. I couldn't take my eyes off him. I managed to open the conversation and before long had asked this handsome boy to Dick's apartment. His name was Chuck Knight, and we got along very well, especially sexually. We began seeing each other but only on weekends.

I invited him to my parents' home for Christmas dinner. After we had finished dinner, we went to a party in Queens to which Johnny had invited us. I wore a red sweater that Johnny had given me for Christmas, and when we arrived, Johnny was also wearing a red sweater that I had given him. We both laughed, took pictures, and had a good time. Later, Chuck and I went home and made babies. Although I liked him, I felt it was best to play it cool for a change. It would work out better, I thought, just seeing each other off and on, which we did for some time with no serious attachments on either part.

As New Year's Eve approached once again, our thoughts were on what to do. "Let's have a bottle party," someone suggested.

"Again?" echoed another.

"Why not? You know that on New Year's everyone will come as long as there's a place to hold it."

The decision was made, and the party set at Eric's apartment. Who else? He was the only one with a place large enough.

He was now living in a loft-apartment on Cooper Union on the East Side. The next step was to clean up the attic and move the unnecessary things to the back to make room for dancing and people. It was dusty and needed painting badly, but no one seemed to care. We dusted and swept and had the place looking halfway decent by 6:00 P.M. the evening before.

Phone calls were made and invitations verbally given in bars. We told whoever wanted to come that they could bring a friend as long as they brought their own liquor. So, 1956–57 started with early arrivals.

"Gee, I'm sorry, there's no music and little ice. You're early!" I told them. "We'll just have to listen to the radio until the records and phonograph get here." They said they didn't mind and mixed themselves drinks.

When Helenmae arrived and had started up the stairs, we saw about ten people coming in behind her. We asked who they were. "I don't know," she said, grinning. "They just followed me. I'm so popular!"

Around ten o'clock we had about fifteen people, and still George and Joe hadn't arrived. I called them and told them to hurry, as people were arriving and the ice was very low. They arrived about twenty minutes later. The dancing started, and everyone seemed to be enjoying themselves. About 11:45, with almost a full house, Johnny and his lover along with some of their friends arrived. By this time, I wasn't feeling any pain and didn't care who knew it. There were so many people I knew and couldn't get to talk with. It seemed like a bar on the weekend. Even with the large loft, which ran the complete length of the building, there was an overflow downstairs in the three large rooms.

Midnight arrived, and amidst the shouting and singing, George emerged from behind the drapes we had set up in the rear to store what we didn't want seen, carrying a large tray with seven or eight glasses and a bottle of champagne. "Well, it's the start of another year. Jennie is dead, long live—" He paused. "Long live—oh shit, long live Gloria." Everyone roared at the name that popped into his head.

After the champagne and arrival of still more people, George retreated once again to the back and went behind the drapes. I went back to ask him what was wrong.

"Nothing. I just don't feel up to a party tonight."

"Anything on your mind, George? Care to talk about it?"

"No, nothing, just don't feel like being with a big crowd tonight, nothing more."

I thought it best to leave him alone and returned to the party. About 4 A.M. the people slowly started leaving. Those left decided to go for coffee. Helenmae said her feet were bothering her and was sorry she had worn high heels. I offered her my shoes, and at first she thought I was joking, but I was high, as was everyone else, so we exchanged. We laughed all the way to the restaurant, she in my loafers and I in her black heels. No one seemed to notice!

This was the way 1957 started for me, a year which was to change many things for me, although at the time I wasn't aware of it. We talked about the shoe incident for some time, and whenever it was mentioned, we always had a good laugh.

TEN

Toward the end of January I took a night job in addition to my regular job, with the hope of clearing up some bills. It was in a travel agency from six to midnight, five days a week, and sometimes overtime on Saturday. Working so late made it impossible to go all the way home to the Bronx, and staying with Joe and George would have been an inconvenience for them. The man in whose apartment I had dressed on Thanksgiving told me he was moving, and I took his apartment. There wasn't any furniture, so Joe gave me a cot. At least I had something to sleep on. I ordered a love seat, two chairs to match, an end table, and coffee table. The furniture arrived, and still the four-room apartment seemed empty. I had plans to fix it up and stay there after I left my night job, which I had hoped would be soon as my bills were lower because working two jobs was extremely tiresome.

One night when I returned from work, I discovered my lock didn't work, for some reason. I didn't know what to do. The apartment next to mine was vacant, and therefore I couldn't get in to go through the fire escape. I decided to call a policeman and explain the situation, which I did, and we then decided to try the superintendent and explain to him. He wouldn't answer his door. "That's not my problem," he said. "What do you mean by waking me at this hour?" He was a nasty son of a bitch, and I felt like banging down the door.

"I happen to work nights," I said.

"Some work," he yelled back.

The officer demanded he open the door, and still he refused. We finally woke the people above me, and after many apologies, I went through the fire escape and into my apartment. The following Sunday I returned to the apartment and had another run-in with the nasty super. I decided it would be hopeless living there for two years as my lease stated.

Fortunately, it didn't become effective until April 1st, and it was now the 27th of March. I engaged a mover the following Saturday and an electrician to remove the refrigerator and gas heater. I was determined to get out of the apartment so that the super couldn't get in touch with the agent until the following Monday. Saturday I had everything removed and went to the super's apartment to return the keys and have the last laugh. He wasn't home, so the last laugh, after all, was on me! I left the keys at the base of his door and left.

I left the furniture at a friend's place, and the following week had it transferred to my parents' home. I now felt everything I tried to do was in vain. Instead of helping pay my bills, I had gotten deeper into debt via the apartment, furniture, etc. I didn't know what to do. I quit the night job a week later, even though I knew I shouldn't. At my regular day job, things weren't going too well either. The work was piling up, so I asked for a raise and was refused because we were unionized and only given raises every two years. At this point, I had had it, so I sent in my resignation, effective May 17. It was now May 3. I had hoped that by giving notice they would reconsider and give me a raise. However, I was wrong! The company said nothing, although I assumed they knew my reason for leaving.

The following Sunday I went to church, and after returning to Joe and George's apartment, I learned from George's friend Tim that they had left for brunch in the Village, and I was to meet them.

As I was changing, the phone rang, and I answered it. The voice on the other end was soft and pleasant. "George?" it said.

"No, I'm sorry, he's not here. Can I take a message?"

"Yes, this is Sal. Tell him I called."

Sal! I thought as he said his name. George had mentioned him. He had been seeing him but wasn't that interested, although Sal was. He told me that Sal was just my type: Italian, about my size, young, and very good-looking. All this was going through my mind as he spoke.

"Okay, I'll tell him. He's in the Village with some friends, and I'm on my way to meet him. I'll give him your message," I said.

"Who's this?" he asked.

"Tom," I replied.

We talked for a few minutes, general conversation, then he asked me what I looked like, and I tried to explain as best I could. He asked if I would mind if he came with me to meet George, and I said it would be fine. We arranged to meet an hour later, as he had just gotten up. I hung up the phone and said to Tim, "That was Sal. He sounds very nice, my dear!"

"He is nice, Tom, you'll love him. I saw him for a few minutes once when I was with George, and he's a doll."

"Really? Humm—well, we'll see!" My interest was growing.

An hour later I left the apartment to meet Sal. We had told each other what we were wearing so it would be easy for each of us to recognize the other. I saw a dark-haired, rather straight-looking boy standing on the corner. *That must be him,* I said to myself. *Boy, Tim wasn't kidding, he's gorgeous!*

It was Sal, and after our introductions we went for coffee. We made the usual small talk, trying to feel each other out. He told me how lonely he was, and that he wanted to meet someone and settle down. He told of his past love affairs, and how upset they had made him. I remained silent (for a change) most of the time and let him do the talking, all the while thinking, *Boy, if there was a chance, could I ever go for you!*

After coffee, we started slowly walking to the Village to meet

George. Suddenly, he said, "You're very nice, Tom. You seem so understanding. I hope we'll be good friends."

"Thanks, Sal. I hope so, too!"

When we arrived at the bar, George and the others weren't there, and I asked a waiter if they had been there.

"You're a little late coming out of church, aren't you?" He smiled.

As usual, all I could do was blush and agree. We left and started looking in several bars, finally locating them in a bar on Eighth Street. I was sure that George would be surprised at my being with Sal, but when we entered, he didn't blink an eye. Later I asked, "Aren't you surprised, I mean, my coming in with him?"

"Surprised?" he said. "When you first came in, I couldn't even think of his name. What is it?"

"Sal, you idiot!"

"Of course, isn't that the funniest? This drink must be stronger than I thought!"

After a few drinks with the crowd, we left and went to another restaurant and talked more. Some time later, we returned to the apartment of Dick Dawson, a friend of Joe's whom I had met before and had become friendly with. He had taken an apartment in Joe's building and given me a set of keys. We weren't there very long when we started making love. Later I told him I had to go to Brooklyn that evening to visit a woman who used to work with me who recently had had a baby, and would meet him when I returned. We made a date for 12:30 that evening. He left, I changed, and went to Brooklyn.

We met later, and I told him I would like to spend the night at his place. He was more than willing, and we had hardly gotten in the door before we were in bed and making love. After that, we saw each other almost nightly. I thought I was beginning to fall in love with him, for the first time since Bill Lopez.

Things were going nicely, I thought. *I have someone I think*

I love, I'm leaving my job with the hopes of finding a better one, and my parents are buying a home on Long Island. How wonderful it's going to be. We talked of the future and what we would do.

However, Sal didn't seem to return the affection in the way I was hoping, and it upset me very much. One evening after we had been to a movie, I left him and took the subway to the Bronx. I was not feeling in the best of spirits and stood in the doorway between the cars of the train, reading the paper. I read an article about a woman who had a spring inserted in her heart, and the operation was a success. I always had a weak stomach, and after reading this it didn't help. I began to feel dizzy and felt I was going to faint. As the train pulled into the 125th Street station, I felt myself slipping. The light summer jacket I was carrying fell on the tracks, and a passenger helped me to the platform. As he was helping me, I seemed to come out of the dizziness and felt a bit better. I thanked him and sat down on a bench as a train man got my jacket. It was covered with dirt and grease. I was worried! Why should I feel this way when basically I felt fine? Was it jaundice again? The last time I had fainted on the subway was a warning. Next day I told Sal what had happened, and he was upset and told me to go to the doctor. I went, and, fortunately, there was nothing physically wrong.

"Do you worry much?" the doctor asked.

"Yes, as a matter of fact, I do."

I told him about my leaving my job and the fact I had to look for another. He finally said, "Between the warm weather and you leaving work, you're probably a mess of nerves, nothing more. Just try to take it easy. I'll give you a prescription for some pills to calm you down. Everything will be all right!"

I felt better as I left the office. The pills did help, although I was still worried. With Sal on the scene, my worries were even greater.

Everyone warned me that he was too young, but like

anyone who thinks they're in love. I wouldn't listen. I had to find out for myself. I realized he was young, just how young I didn't know, and questioned him several times, but he wouldn't tell me. He said, "I never tell people how old I am—does it matter to you?"

"Not really, but I would like to know, just the same. I know you're younger than me, and, let's fact it, honey, I'll be twenty-seven next month."

"Twenty-seven! You certainly don't look it. You could be taken for nineteen or twenty," he said.

"Oh, come on, now, let's not get carried away! I may look younger than I am, but nineteen or twenty, no way! Twenty-three or twenty-four, maybe!"

"That's only how you think you look to others, but, hon, believe me, you look much younger than you are!"

"Let's drop the whole subject. I get very nudgy when I think about age," I said, and it was dropped.

A week or so later we were to meet George and Tim at a dancing bar. We arrived at the bar and ordered drinks. As I started to pay for them, the manager came over and asked Sal for his identification. He said he didn't have it with him and had left it at home. He was asked to leave. I felt embarrassed, not only for myself and Sal but for George and Tim, but they just shrugged the whole matter off.

Later, when we were alone, I again asked him how old he was. "Don't give me this crap about leaving your ID at home or that you can't find it. The reason you can't find it is because you aren't old enough to have one. Am I right?"

He lowered his eyes and said nothing. So I continued questioning him. "You said your birthday is in September. That means you're only going to be eighteen this September, doesn't it?"

"Is it that important, Tom?" he finally said.

"Of course not, hon, but why didn't you just tell me, and

we could have avoided this. We'll just stay out of the bars until you're old enough and have a card. What's so bad about that?"

"I was afraid if I told you, you wouldn't want me around," he said.

"I want you around, don't worry," I whispered as I grabbed him and pulled him down on the bed.

Days later I again noticed he had a worried expression on his face and asked what was wrong.

"I don't know, Tom, all I know is that I've got to get some money. How, I don't really know, and yet I do know. There's only one way!"

He didn't have to go any further. I suspected, and my heart almost stopped! "No, Sal, not that way! I like you too much to see you sell yourself like a common prostitute!"

"But, hon, it's the only way. It will only be for a short time, and then we'll have enough money to do what we want. I have the body for it, and last year I made over two grand, but like a fool I spent every cent of it."

"Two grand! Oh, Sal, how could you? That's about the lowest thing I've ever heard of."

"Is it so wrong to want nice things and a place to enjoy them?" he asked.

"I'm not questioning the fact that it's nice to have money. It's wonderful, if you work for it honestly."

"Tom, it's the only way for me. Remember everything I do will be for us."

Shades of Billy Lopez, I thought to myself. *History does repeat itself.* But to him I said, "Sure, but you know every time you go out with someone, I'll sit home and almost die!"

"Think about it baby, please," he pleaded.

"I'll think about it," I said, "but I still don't like the idea."

I did think about it, and the more I did the more upset I became. I finally thought it would be better to call the whole thing off. I didn't know if I was really in love or if it was just infatuation, but I did know I would be happier not knowing what he was doing; although at the same time not being with him was even worse.

I tried to explain why I wanted to call it off. "It isn't that I don't love you. I'm really not sure! One thing I do know, and that is that you don't love me or care for me the way I do. If you did, you wouldn't be doing what you're planning."

"You're right, Tom, I don't love you, but give me time, I think I could," he said. "Wait about a month and see what happens!"

"A month sounds a bit silly, but, okay, I'll give it a try."

Later that evening as he was dressing, he told me he was going for an interview as a waiter in a gay bar. I questioned the fact he was so well dressed.

"You usually wear sports clothes, why the sudden switch?" I asked. "Are you sure you don't have a date with one of your you know whats?"

"*If* I had a date, I'd tell you! I've nothing to hide now. I'm going for an interview, and that's all!"

"Okay, then call me tonight and let me know how you made out. I'll be up till midnight." I still didn't believe him and was sure that he had a "date" for financial reasons.

He didn't call, and I was so furious, I wouldn't call him. Something was definitely wrong! It bothered me, but what could I do?

The following Friday, the waiting got to be too much, and I called, and we arranged to meet. He returned the ID he had borrowed, and when he did I knew for sure it was the end of us.

"You don't have to tell me, Sal, I know. You decided it wasn't worth it to wait, or have you found another heart to break? How thankful I am you didn't get around to breaking mine. Just a little crack perhaps, but not completely broken," I said, smiling, knowing full well I was lying and that he knew it as well.

He smiled with that beautiful smile of his that made me

want to kiss him right there in the restaurant. "You always seem to be one step ahead of me. Yes, you're right, I have met someone. Someone I like very much, but now the shoe is on the other foot. The love and affection I didn't show you is being done to me by Bill. That's his name."

Where have I heard this before? I said to myself.

"He treats me like I treated you, but when we're alone, I know he cares. Just the same, I'm moving in tonight."

"You mean to say, if I hadn't called, today, I wouldn't have known about this?"

"Of course not. I was going to call you!"

"When? Next year?"

"Don't be ridiculous. You know I'd have called."

"Well, all I can say is that I certainly wish you every happiness. Don't misunderstand me, I'm not jealous of your newfound love, just a blt sorry for you both, especially him. You're so young and have so much to learn. I don't mean sexually, you know that backwards, but so much to learn that only experience and years will teach. I wish I could explain better, but I can't."

"I think I understand. But we'll still be friends and see each other from time to time," he said.

"I hope so, Sal!" At this point I was trying to hold back the tears and had to think of something to end the conversation. "Look, I've got to leave. I have to meet George," I lied. I just wanted to get out of there before I really let go. "Have you a phone where you're going?"

"Not yet, but we expect one this week. I'll keep in touch, hon." With that we left the restaurant and said good-bye.

On the subway to Joe's apartment, I thought the world was ending for me. *Do I love that little stinker? What am I going to do now?*

That evening Tim and I went out drinking.

"Tim, I don't know whether I love him or not. Only thing I

do know is that I have this terrible lonesome feeling I can't explain. But I suppose it's better this way. I'll get over it eventually. I just wish I could sit down and cry and get it out of my system."

"Try to forget it, Tom," he said. "It's probably better this way!"

"But, Tim, why is it so wrong for me to find happiness? Other people do but never me. I've more or less resolved myself to the fact that no matter what I do, where I go, or who I meet, I'll never find the happiness I really want in gay life. Since I've taken this attitude, it's a bit better, but it still hurts."

"Come on, Tom, let's have another drink and forget about the whole messy affair. Say, look at that doll over in the corner," he said.

I smiled. My eyes had started to water up, and I knew why he had just said that. *I'll go along with him,* I thought. *He's just trying to help me forget.* "Where, Tim, where's the doll?"

ELEVEN

What had the future to hold for me now? I was out of work, and nothing seemed to be coming my way. I refused to go to an agency and pay so much money for a position and then possibly not like it and leave, losing the money I had spent and could ill afford. I placed an ad for a social secretary position in a motion picture trade paper, but nothing came of it. They had placed the ad free of charge, so I hadn't lost anything.

Joe and I decided to go to Atlantic City and look for work there, he as an elevator operator and I as a waiter. Although I had never done waiter work, I figured I could get by. The season wasn't open yet, so neither of us secured anything. Disheartened, we returned to New York and continued looking for jobs.

I looked in the papers daily. By now they were like my Bible. Finally I saw an ad for a stencil typist and applied. When I saw the amount of people that had applied, I thought I wouldn't stand a chance. Surely someone else was more qualified than I. Nevertheless, I took the test, and they told me they would be in touch. I assumed they were just being polite and continued looking for a job. The next day, the phone rang, and I had the job if I wanted it. I was to report for work the following Monday. I was delighted! True, it wasn't exactly what I wanted, but it was a job. I had been out of work only a month, but it seemed much longer.

The day before I was to report for work, Eric got married. Most everyone at the reception were old friends and others I hadn't seen for some time. I enjoyed myself, as I'm sure the others did, but couldn't stay too late because of the new job the following day. I wanted to have a clear head when I arrived.

The job turned out to be completely different and much easier than I had anticipated. There were times when we were very busy, but most of the time it was extremely slow. I was bored, but it was a job, and I was being paid, so why complain?

A few weeks later was the Fourth of July. We had planned, as usual, to go to Atlantic City. I realized I wouldn't get a vacation that year, so weekends would have to do. As it turned out, no one could make it! Joe still wasn't working, Dick had to work that particular weekend, and George had already left for Daytona Beach on his vacation. I decided to go alone, knowing I would run into people I knew.

From the moment I arrived, I ran into old friends and wasn't alone very long. I had no trouble meeting new people since I was alone, so to speak. Saturday night, the night before I was to return to New York, I was talking with a friend in the bar when he suddenly said, "Honey, did that number ever give you the eye!"

"What number?" I asked.

"The dark-haired beauty sitting by the entrance to the men's room," he replied.

I turned to look and saw what I now considered "my type": Italian, about nineteen or twenty, jet-black hair, big brown eyes, and a terrific tan.

"Don't be silly, Howard. I know that guy from New York. I've seen him there dozens of times."

"Could be, but he's from Philly, and he was giving you the eye. Wanna meet him?"

At this point, between the liquor and the thought that someone as good-looking as this could be interested in me, I agreed. We were shortly in conversation, and from all appearances, he was more plastered than I was.

"You'll have to excuse me, Tom, but I've had quite a bit to

drink tonight, and I'm starting to feel it. In fact, I don't feel so good."

"Would you like to go for coffee?" I asked. "Maybe it'll help!"

He agreed, and after coffee we went to my hotel. We had just gotten in the door, when he excused himself and went to the bathroom. This continued for almost half an hour. Finally, when we were in bed, I asked if he felt any better now that he had gotten most of it up.

"I feel much better," he said and looked at me so affectionately that I leaned over and kissed him. We grew passionate.

Suddenly, he sat up in the bed and looked at me. "You know, this is all an act. I mean, my being so drunk!"

"An act? What do you mean?"

"Well, when I first saw you, I dug you the most, but you didn't pay any attention to me, so I thought if I pretended to be drunk maybe you'd notice me."

"Do you think you have to be drunk to have people find you interesting?" I asked. "You're a beautiful man. You don't have to pull anything to attract attention."

He smiled and said nothing. He leaned over and kissed me. Nothing more needed to be said. A while later, we were fast asleep.

Next morning, we had breakfast and went to the beach. About three o'clock, I suggested we leave and get ready for the cocktail hour. After dressing, we met, had something to eat, and went to the bar. We didn't stay very long because I was leaving that evening at eight o'clock, and we wanted to spend the rest of the time together. We made love in Bill's hotel room the rest of the afternoon, and before we parted he told me he loved me. The thought had crossed my mind, too (how easily we all fell in love in those early days—the right look, word or action and it was Lala land, no?). I gave him my address, and he promised to write the following week. All the way home on the bus I thought of the wonderful weekend I just had had, but especially the hours I had spent with Bill.

I waited for the letter, which never came. Finally, two weeks later, some friends and I returned to Atlantic City for another weekend. All I wanted to know was why he hadn't written. If there was someone else or he had changed his mind, fine, but not knowing was what upset me most.

After we changed, we went to the bar. I found out he wasn't in town and felt lost. There was nothing to do, and I wasn't going to waste the weekend, so I met a few people and had a couple of affairs.

Another two weeks and still no letter. Once again I made the trip, hoping to find the answer. Dick Dawson had never been to Atlantic City and decided to go with me. After changing, we headed for the beach. We had left New York early, so the whole day was ahead of us.

"How do you like AC, Dick?" I asked after we had settled on the beach.

"From what I've seen so far, great! No wonder you come down here so often!"

"It is nice, but every once in awhile, like everything else, it bores me. I swear it's the last time I'll come here, but just like the song, I keep coming back. Must have some sort of hold on me!"

I looked around the beach. It was Saturday, and there were many people. I saw several familiar faces, and we exchanged greetings.

"My God!" cried Dick. "The way you keep saying hello to people, one would think you had lived here all your life!"

I smiled and said, "If you were down here as much as I am, you'd know twice the people I do!"

"Sure, just like that!"

"It's not hard to meet people here, Dick. Most of them are very friendly, and we see each other no matter where we go.

There aren't that many places here. We either run into one another on the beach, at the cocktail hour, at dinner, or just strolling on the boardwalk. First, it's just a smile or nod of recognition, then, before you know it, one day you're talking and bang, you've another new friend."

"Friend? You mean to tell me you haven't been to bed with any of the people you just said hello to?" Dick asked.

"A few! Damn few and far between. Most of them are just bar acquaintances, not bedmates."

"U-huh," he said with a sly look, "I see!"

"No, you don't see, you dizzy ass. What do you think I am, anyway, a whore? No, don't answer that!" I smiled and continued looking around the beach.

"What time does the cocktail hour start, Tom?" he asked.

"About four, but I usually don't get there till—" My thoughts were interrupted as I saw two men crossing the sand, going toward the refreshment stand. One of the boys looked at me and smiled. I returned his smile and watched him until he was out of sight.

"Who's that?" Dick asked.

"I don't know, but he's a doll! Know something, Dick? I'm going to go to bed with him tonight!"

"Yeah! You don't know who he is, but you're going to bed with him!" Dick smiled.

"Well, I can dream, can't I? Besides, you never can tell! I probably won't even see him tonight!"

"As I was saying, what time does the cocktail hour start?"

"I'm sorry, Dick. Usually about four, but we don't get there till about five. I hate to be too early. Like to make an entrance. In fact, while I'm thinking of it, I'd better leave early and change!"

"Change! Why? What's wrong with what you're wearing?" he asked.

"Nothing, but I always go home before, take a shower, shave if I need it, and change my bathing suit. I look and feel refreshed when I get there. Can't hurt, you know! A girl always has to look her best."

"I suppose it can't, but aren't you being just a little too much?"

"Who cares? Don't kid yourself. A lot of others do exactly the same."

Dick shook his head as if to say, "Well, I think you're all crazy."

When the cocktail hour ended, we left and had dinner. We ate in a restaurant that was primarily gay. The waiters were also gay. As ours approached, he eyed Dick with a hungry glare and said, "Your orders, please."

After he took our orders and left, I said to Dick, "Seems sort of interested in you, doesn't he?"

"Who?" he asked.

"The waiter. Haven't you noticed the way he looked at you? He's not that bad. You could do worse, you know!"

Dick didn't seem to hear my last remark and continued sipping his drink while looking around the restaurant. (If I hadn't mentioned it before, Dick was an extremely attractive man with blond hair and brown eyes about an inch or two taller than me and nicely built.)

After dinner, we took a walk on the boardwalk, and I pointed out spots of interest to him and told him of several places he might find interesting later if he didn't meet anyone. We returned to the hotel and decided to rest for a few hours before going out for the evening.

At the hotel, I undressed and got into bed. I was half asleep when Dick returned from the bathroom. He quietly undressed and eased himself into the double bed next to me.

The alarm rang and I sprang upright in bed, looked over at Dick who was just beginning to wake up, and said, "Time to get up and make ourselves beautiful for the boys." I laughed, hitting Dick squarely on his rear.

He turned and smiled. "What time is it?"

"Ten-thirty. By the time we're dressed and out of here, it'll be time enough."

We each took our time dressing, and when we were ready, I asked Dick where he would like to go first. He said it didn't matter. I showed him where I usually put the room key in case we were separated, turned out the light, and we left the hotel.

We entered the bar, ordered our drinks, and I ran into people I knew. After I introduced Dick, we all chatted for awhile, and Dick strolled to the side leaving us to our conversation. A few minutes later, I joined him.

"There's what a number over there that has been giving me the eye," he said.

"Well, in that case, I'll leave you. Good luck—you know where the keys are!"

I left him and walked over to the railing and propped myself against it. The jukebox was playing. As I looked around, it wasn't until I had turned my body slightly to my left that I saw the boy who had smiled at me earlier on the beach. We exchanged glances and finally smiled at one another. I wanted to say something, but I didn't know what. Then several people entered the bar and pushed pass us. In doing so, we had to move slightly. As more people entered, we were pushed closer. I smiled, and he returned the smile.

"Getting quite crowded, isn't it?" he said.

"Certainly is!"

"My name's Johnny Parks. What's yours?"

I told him my name, and our conversation was routine for some time. I wanted to ask him home but decided to wait. Finally I suggested we have coffee (the old standby, at this point), and he agreed. I said good night to Dick, and we left the bar.

After coffee, we went to my hotel. As I was taking off my

clothes, Johnny grabbed and kissed me. "I've been wanting to do that since I first saw you," he said.

"So did I. How come you were so shy on the beach and in the bar tonight?" I finally asked.

"Well, you can ask any of my friends if you don't believe this, but you're the first person I've gone home with since I've been coming to the shore. I just don't like going with people just for the sake of sex," he said. This, of course, was a lot of bull, which I would find out many years later.

"You mean there's something else?" I said, trying to be humorous.

He smiled and said, "You know what I mean!"

"Yes, I think so, but how come you decided on me? Am I so different from others?"

"I don't know why. Just seeing and talking to you made me want to be with you. You've that way about you. I like you, Tom. I think you're very nice."

"I like you, too, Johnny."

Only the sound of the alarm clock ticking was heard in the quiet of the room. When I awoke later, I looked over at Johnny, who was looking at me.

"Dick hasn't come home yet!" He smiled.

"Probably met someone. What time is it?"

"Four-thirty and time for me to be going," he said.

"No, stay please. Most likely he won't be home tonight. Spend the night. If he does come, he comes, if he doesn't, well—"

We held each other and kissed again. We talked for awhile, and dawn found us at the bottom of the bed, both asleep with peaceful expressions on our faces. Dick hadn't come home at all that evening.

After I got up, showered, and shaved, I woke Johnny. "Time to get up, sleepy head. It's 11:30!"

"Hummmmm! I hate to get up. Come here!" he said.

"What?"

"This!" He grabbed me and pulled me to the bed.

"So early in the morning? Really!" I said, smiling.

"I wasn't thinking about that. Can't I kiss you if I want to?"

"Honey, you can kiss me any time or place you care to."

Before he left, we exchanged addresses, and he promised (as did many before him) to write. Although I liked Johnny, I still wanted to know what had happened to Bill, so the search continued.

I began hearing stories about Bill. One was that he was underage and had been sent out of town. Another placed him in New York on various weekends. *If he was in New York, why didn't he call me?* I thought. I was puzzled and confused.

As I was about to give the whole thing up as a lost cause, Dick and I decided to go for a few drinks before dinner and the trip back home. After we got our drinks, we stood talking and looking around the room. Then I saw him sitting in the same seat where I had first met him—Bill.

I shook, and Dick noticed and asked what was wrong. "You look as white as a ghost. What happened?" he asked, genuinely concerned.

"It's Bill over there in the corner with those girls. He hasn't seen me yet, and I'm completely wrecked."

Almost as I said that, he got up to use the men's room, and as he started to pass me, I managed to say, "What's the matter Bill, don't you say hello to an old friend?" Such a corny line, but I had to say something.

He turned and smiled. "Hi, Tom. How are you?"

"What's wrong Bill, why didn't you write?" I finally blurted out.

"I'll tell you in a minute. I'll be right back." And he left.

"How do you like that, Dick," I said. "He won't be back. I just know it!"

About ten minutes later he did return, and we sat down.

"I lost your address. Besides, I heard you told someone what we did."

"That's nonsense! I don't go around discussing my sex life with *anyone!*"

"Well, how did they know?" he asked.

"I don't know, Bill. Probably just some guesswork to trick you. You know how some queens are!"

We talked a while longer, and I gave him my address again. He told me he still felt the same, and that he would be in New York in two weeks and would call me the Thursday before he came. I told him I'd be expecting him, and we parted once again. I was happy again! I finally knew the answer, I least I thought I did, but my happiness was to be short-lived, as were so many of my affairs lately.

I didn't receive a letter, and this time I was furious. *There's no excuse for it this time,* I thought. *How stupid can I be? I suppose it's because he's so terribly young. What an ass I've been.*

A week later I decided to call Sal. I owed him a call and wanted to know how everything was.

"Gee, I'm glad you called, Tom. It's been such a long time. I'd like to see you some time. What are you doing tomorrow?" he asked.

"Nothing special that I know of. Why?"

"Well, I thought maybe we could meet and take in a movie or something. I've so much to tell you."

"Okay, call me tomorrow afternoon and we can make arrangements."

He called as promised, and we met downtown. It was a lovely evening, so we decided not to go to a movie but to take a walk instead. We walked and talked until my feet and mouth were exhausted. He hadn't been getting along with his new friend as he had expected and was upset. I suspected this the day before when he asked to meet me.

We had walked so much that we found ourselves at Dick's apartment, and I suggested we go up for awhile. My feet were tired, and I knew Dick wouldn't be home, so we could talk privately.

In Dick's apartment we talked more and kept looking at each other. Before long we were in each other's arms.

"How I've missed this," he said.

"Me, too," I agreed.

"Look, Tom, I don't know how to say this, but suppose, just suppose we were to get back together again, how would you feel about it?"

"Back together? I don't know! I do like you, but I'm not in love with you. I could be, but I don't want to be hurt like the last time. I just couldn't take it again," I told him.

"No, I mean on your terms," he said.

"Well, let me think about it. I'll let you know for sure!"

"Okay, hon!" he answered.

We made love, and I didn't have to think about it. I still cared but knew I didn't dare let him know how much. He had walked all over me once; I didn't want it a second time.

We saw each other almost every night for about a week. Then it started again! He wouldn't call or see me. One Friday when I knew George and Joe would be away and I could have the apartment to myself, I called him to tell him not to make any plans for the following night. He said okay and that he would call me the next day, but, of course, didn't. I kept calling him all evening but still no answer. *Now, where can that bitch be?* I said to myself. *Screw it, I'm going out!*

I called a friend and met him. Later we were invited to a party, but I didn't feel like going. As much as I liked Sal, my thoughts were still on Bill, so I went uptown to a bar I knew he went to with the hope of seeing him.

As I was waiting for the bartender to give me my drink, I saw Bill heading for the back. We just looked at each other but didn't speak. I wanted to, but when I saw him, something stopped me. He put both his hands on my waist and gently moved me to the side so he could pass, smiling as he did so. I turned and gave him a slight smile, too. After I got my drink, I went to the back of the bar to watch the dancing and met some people I knew. Bill was close by, and still not a word passed between us. One of the people I was with asked me if I had been downstairs. I told him I hadn't, and he suggested we go. We went to a dark corner of the bar, and a buzzer was pressed. We opened the door and went down a long flight of stairs. "Very mysterious," I said, "and very interesting; almost like a story or a movie." When we arrived downstairs, I looked around. I liked it. It was different! I knew George would love it.

We danced for a while and ran into more people we knew. Later, I went upstairs to look for a friend to tell him something and again ran into Bill. I had taken off my sweater because it was very warm and Bill, noticing this, said "Why the gay change?"

I looked at him, ignoring the question. "I'm looking for a friend, but in this crowd it's impossible." Then I smiled at him and went back downstairs. That was the last time we ever saw each other, and I never did find out what all the problems were concerning him.

Next day I called Sal. I wanted to see him and finally end our affair. As usual, he wasn't home (remember, in those days we didn't have answering machines yet). I decided to go to a Forty-second Street movie, which was a thing I had been doing quite a bit, as of late.

While cruising around the movie, I met a young Puerto Rican boy. During our conversation, he told me his name was Bobby Garcia. Of course, at this time in life I didn't know it, but Bobby was to become a very close friend in the years to come. I asked him if he would like to leave with me, but he said he couldn't. So, after talking a while longer, we parted, and I continued looking around, found someone, and left the theater.

When I finally did get in touch with Sal, a few days later, he told me he had a lot on his mind and wanted to be alone. He said he was going to Fire Island for the weekend and would call me the following week. I didn't hear from him for some time after that, and, in a way, was happier for it.

I received a card from Johnny Parks, asking why I hadn't written. It seemed funny to me because I had written, and most likely our letters had crossed in the mail. I answered his card and told him I wasn't going to AC that weekend as planned and suggested he come to New York. A few days later he called and told me he was coming and asked that I meet him at Penn Station. If we missed each other for any reason, we were to meet at the information booth on the upper level.

"Who's Johnny?" asked George when I told him he was coming.

"A guy I met a few weeks ago in AC when I was down with Dick. I thought I told you about him. He's very nice, quiet, good dresser, and *not* bad looking. I really like him," I told George.

"Here we go again!" he said.

"Now, I didn't say anything like that. I merely said I *liked* him, not loved him. I hardly know the guy!"

"But knowing you, you can be in love with him before you know what hit you!"

"True, George, how very true, but time will tell. I haven't even given it much thought."

"I'll bet you haven't!"

I just smiled.

I arrived at Penn Station at 9:45 P.M. Johnny's train was due at 9:55. I waited for the announcement to come over the loudspeaker and went with other people to the assigned track. After all the passengers were off the train, there was no sign of

Johnny. Thinking I had somehow missed him, I went to the booth as we had planned. He wasn't there!

"If I can't make the 6:04," I recalled our phone conversation, "I'll definitely be on the next train. Find out when it arrives and meet me accordingly."

The next train was due at 11:45, and it was now 10:15. I walked around, had a soda and several cigarettes. At 11:45 I went to the track and still no sign of him. I went again to the information booth, and he wasn't there. I waited fifteen more minutes then had him paged. No response! I realized now something had gone wrong, and that perhaps at the last minute he couldn't make it, so I returned to George's apartment. Johnny Tyler had arrived while I was gone. I told them what had happened and then went to Dick's apartment and called Johnny. His mother told me he hadn't made the 6:04 and would be on the 8:30 train, which arrived in New York about 1:00 A.M. She thanked me for calling and for my concern.

George, Johnny Tyler, and I decided to go for a drink and wait the time out. A little after 1:00 A.M., we drove in Johnny's car to Penn Station and went to the information booth because we were late. As we approached, I saw him and walked ahead of the others. He told me he was sorry for being so late, followed by the usual small talk. He checked his bag, and we drove uptown to a bar. In the car, I thought it best to find out what the weekend would hold and told him that if he wanted to cruise, it would be all right with me.

"I came here to see you, not to cruise," he said.

I couldn't have been more pleased with what he said and moved closer, and we embraced just as George, who was sitting in the front seat with Johnny, looked around.

"She's at it already!" he said jokingly.

We all laughed, and after Johnny parked the car, went into the bar. We stayed for a while, and then Johnny drove us back to Penn Station to pick up Johnny's suitcase, and then back to

Dick's apartment. Dick was spending the weekend at Peter's apartment, someone he had recently met and was now seeing on a permanent basis. Johnny unpacked. Very tired and contented, we both got into bed but didn't get to sleep for some time.

Next morning after breakfast, we went for a walk to the Village, where the art exhibition was being held. We walked for what seemed like hours, and my feet were killing me. I had forgotten about all the walking I had done with Sal and asked Johnny if we could stop and rest for a while.

"Don't tell me you're tired already?" he asked.

"I sure am! Not used to so much walking," I told him.

"Better get used to it, hon. I love to walk!"

"Well, you go right ahead. I'll take a cab and meet you," I said, smiling.

We rested for a few minutes then continued looking at the art show. After we returned to Dick's apartment, I gave Johnny the keys and told him I was going to the Bronx to change clothes and would be back later.

When I arrived back downtown, Johnny went for dinner and I had a cup of coffee. We then returned to the apartment, and Dick had come in with Peter. We had a few beers, and, before long, it was 3:00 A.M. and too late to go anywhere. Dick left with Peter and told me he was spending the night, for which I was grateful.

Sunday was bright and beautiful, and after church we went to the park to take pictures. For some reason they didn't come out, and we were disappointed. Later in the evening, Johnny Tyler and his lover, Fred, came over. Dick and Peter were there, and we all decided to go dancing. George was the only one without a date this particular night, but we all knew he wouldn't be alone for long.

While sitting at the bar later that evening as George and

Johnny were dancing, Johnny Tyler noticed I was wearing a ring he hadn't seen before.

"It's beautiful!" he said. "Where did you get it?"

I smiled and told him that Johnny had given it to me that afternoon.

He leaned over and whispered, "Are you going together?"

"I think so. Ask him—I'm still confused!"

He did ask him, and Johnny said, "I hope so!"

I was really happy the rest of the evening, happier than I'd been in some time. Johnny Tyler noticed it and remarked, "You seem to be at ease with this guy, Tom. It's really wonderful! I've been watching you. You don't seem to act as you did with anyone I've seen you with before. How come?"

"I don't know! All I do know is that when I'm with him, I'm completely contented; not a worry! I don't even mind when he dances with others. Remember how I used to act when I was with someone I liked or thought I liked and someone else would try to make a pass? With Johnny, it seems different!"

"Tom, I hope you're right! If you knew how much I want to see you happy, even half as much as I am right now. We're such good friends, and I want the best for you, as I know you do for me!"

I looked at him and smiled, my eyes almost filling with tears of joy. "Yes," I said softly, "I know, and how thankful I am to have you as a friend. I've told you many times before, but I'll never tire of saying it."

He thanked me, and we just looked at one another as George and Johnny came off the dance floor. Both were exhausted and filled with perspiration. I had worn a sweater, and Johnny changed in the men's room so that he wouldn't catch cold when we left, which would be soon because it was getting late.

We arrived home, he changed again, and came into the living room, where I was listening to the radio and having a cigarette. I asked him what time he was leaving the next day, and he said he wanted to catch the three o'clock because he didn't want to get home too late.

"I wish tomorrow would never come!" I said. "These last three days just flew by."

"I know, and I hate to go back, too, but I'll be back in three weeks. I'll tell you this much: I promise I won't carry on with anyone. I don't want to, now! Besides, there's nothing in my town," he added, smiling.

"So you come to New York for your thrills, eh?" I answered with an expression on my face that told him I was just joking.

"You know better than that. I came because now I have someone to come to."

"You do, Johnny, you do!"

I went to the station to see him off. My heart was sad, and I wanted to kiss him, but of course couldn't. We had to settle for shaking hands and whispering our good-byes. Then he was gone, out of sight for another three weeks. I turned and slowly walked to the subway and took the train home.

A few days later while on my way to work I ran into Bobby Garcia, and we stopped and chatted for a few minutes. I had been invited to a party at a friend's house and asked Bobby if he would like to go. He said he would, and I gave him my phone number and asked him to call. He did during the week, and that Sunday, we went to the birthday party of still another friend of mine, Ray Zimmer.

Bobby was an excellent dancer, and we danced most of the afternoon together. He was very nice but terribly young! *Seventeen!* I thought to myself, *Even if I do have a lover and decided to cheat a bit, seventeen is too much, even for me.* But then I had gone with Sal when he was seventeen, but I was a little younger then. We started calling each other as friends and occasionally he would join us for drinks, having a fake ID card, but we never made love.

Johnny's letters came, and he also called. Before we realized it, the three weeks were gone, and he was back in town. I again met him, and as we exchanged small talk, we almost felt like strangers. In the apartment he unpacked, and we began to embrace.

"Better let me unpack or we'll be here all night." He smiled. "I didn't bring half the things I did the first time. You were right; I don't need them."

We went upstairs to see Joe and watched TV for awhile. George said he was going to Forty-second Street to cruise and see a movie. Johnny and I left and went to the Village, but we were both tired and didn't stay long.

We stopped by again at Joe's and had coffee with him. We were talking when George came in from the movie.

"How were the pickings?" Joe asked.

"Ugh, don't ask! I'm here, aren't I?"

"That bad, eh? Have a cup of coffee," suggested Joe.

"No, I've got to work tomorrow, so if you kids will excuse me, I'm going to bed."

"Well, I guess we'd better be going, too, Joe," I said. "I know you have to work, also. Thanks for the coffee, and I'll see you tomorrow at Helenmae's party."

"Okay, dolls, be good, see you tomorrow!" he said and we left.

"I'll leave it right here by the phone. He's sure to see it! Can't give me no story she didn't see it—"

I recognized the voice but being half-asleep didn't pay much attention. I opened one eye to catch a glimpse of George and Joe leaving the bedroom. They had keys to Dick's apartment, too. Seems everyone did! When I finally woke later, I looked at the phone where Joe had placed the note. It read: "Would you be dolls and do some shopping for me? I have to work and don't know what time I'll be done. I'd appreciate it if you would go to the A & P and pick up some things for the party tonight. The list is on the back. Thanks a million!"

I looked the list over. "Boy, he hasn't left a thing off! Look, Johnny, I'll go with you and pick the things up, then I have to go home. Tomorrow is my sister's birthday, and I promised to get her a dog at the ASPCA, and she'll be disappointed if I don't."

"No, baby, I'll get them, and you go home. It will save time!"

"Sure you don't mind? I mean, I'll go with you! There's quite a bit to get, you know!"

"Not at all. You run along, but first let's have breakfast. I'm starved!"

After breakfast (which was now late afternoon), I took the train home, went to the ASPCA, selected the dog, and returned home, showered, and changed.

"Don't bother with dinner tonight, Mom, I'm staying at Joe's. It's his brother-in-law's birthday, so I'll eat there and stay over," I told her.

When I arrived back at Joe's apartment he was asleep in bed, and Johnny was on the couch watching TV. He said he didn't realize what time it was and had gotten interested in a TV program. I shooed him downstairs, and he showered, changed, and we went out so he could get something to eat. I had a rum collins that sent my head swimming. I had stopped on the way down in a tie shop and selected two ties for Al (Helenmae's husband) as a gift, so there was one less thing we had to do. After Johnny ate, we returned to Joe's apartment to await the guests.

"I didn't know what to get him," I told Helenmae later, "and he can always use ties!"

"I'm sure he'll love them. Thanks, Tom," she replied.

About fifteen people arrived, and the liquor went fast. I had quite a bit to drink and was starting to feel the effects. Knowing how much Johnny disliked my drinking, I said to Dick, "Look, honey, I've had a few too many, so if I start acting silly, kick me or something! Johnny'll have my head if he knew how drunk I am!"

"You don't look it," said Dick. "Are you really drunk?"

"Pissed to the tits, and I'm having a ball."

Dick and Peter smiled, and I returned to the living room. I had suggested going dancing after the party broke up, and, as the guests started leaving, I went downstairs for a few minutes. When I returned most of the guests had already left. Johnny, Peter, Dick, and I took a cab uptown. When the drinks arrived at the table, I insisted on paying for them. I reached for my wallet but didn't have it.

"I must have left my wallet at home, Dick. Loan me some money until tomorrow."

He gave me five dollars, and I paid for the drinks (imagine getting four drinks and a tip for five dollars—what would that cost today?). After the second drink, for which Dick and Peter paid, they told us they were going to the Village and asked if we wanted to come along. I told them no, that we were enjoying ourselves, and that we would see them the next day.

When we arrived back home, I couldn't find my wallet. I was concerned, not for the money but the credit cards and identification I had in it. After Johnny left, he promised to write, and the next day I wrote the Social Security and draft boards for replacements of my cards.

In the weeks that followed I heard from Johnny, and we planned to meet in AC for the drag on November 2nd, which I learned later was cancelled. I called him and told him it was now being held on October 28. He said he couldn't make it but would be in touch. I had to attend a wedding with my mother the week before, so he couldn't come to New York. Things were a bit mixed-up, but we would work them out.

Early Saturday morning, Joe, Stan, Ellie (a friend of Joe and Helenmae's) and I took off in Ellie's car for AC. George had to work that day, and he, Helenmae, and Al would arrive that evening. George had set my hair the night before and told me not to take it out until I reached the hotel in AC. I obeyed faithfully and wore a cap in the car over the curlers. On the way down we stopped to have something to eat. I had to wait in the car because of my hair. I waited awhile and finally had to use the men's room. I dashed from the car, through the dining room, and into the men's room. While there, two men looked at me very strangely and with good reason, I thought, although I had taken the pins out in the front so it didn't look that ridiculous. Back in the car, I read a magazine and waited for the others to finish eating. When they returned, they brought me a hamburger, coffee, and doughnuts, which I munched on as we continued our trip. We arrived at 5:15 and proceeded directly to the hotel. our accommodations taken care of, it was now dinnertime. I took more clips out, rearranged the cap, and asked Joe how I looked.

"Like an idiot woman!" he remarked with a smile.

I gave him a frown followed by a smile, and we left for the restaurant. While there, several men came in, looked at up and smiled. "See you tonight," they said in low voices.

After dinner, Joe and Ellie went for a walk, and Stan and I returned to the hotel while I shaved, took a bath, and began to get ready. About 9:30, George, Helenmae, and Al arrived. Then it began, running from room to room, borrowing this and that, and helping each other with our outfits. George combed me out for about twenty minutes, sprayed my hair, and said, "Okay, honey, out!"

At 1:30 A.M. we were all ready and set out in the rain for the bar where the drag was being held. When we arrived, the Grand March was already over, and as we entered, every head in the place turned. I was wearing a wine colored, see-through gown that Ellie had made for me, George was in a black and blue bathing suit, and Joe in a similar showgirl outfit. One guy came over to us and said, "Honey, you can tell you queens are from New York. You're all so gorgeous!"

We smiled and thanked him and asked how he knew we were from New York.

"By the way you're all dressed and carry yourselves. The kids down here don't go in for it that much, cock-a-doodle-do, any drag'll do, sort of thing."

We laughed and continued talking. Suddenly, a voice shouted over the noise of the bar, "Could I go for you—WOW!" We all looked up to see a nice-looking young man, quite high, coming over to us. He grabbed me by the arm and said, "Baby, are you for real?"

I stood up, towering over him by two or three inches (he must have been short, but then I was in three-inch heels). Looking down at him, I said, "What do you mean, am I for real? Can't you tell?"

"Sure, honey, but what I want to know is where the hell did you get that figure? It's better than a lot of girls I know."

"Thanks very much," I said coldly, "but that's for me to know, and not for you to find out!"

"Okay, okay, honey, just wanted to let you know I think you're tops."

I gave him a weak smile and sat back down, as the man returned to his table.

Shortly, the manager of the bar, who was also in drag, wanted us to pose for a picture. "Wait till this record is over and then go by the band, and we'll take pictures of you all together," he told us.

When the record was over, we assembled by the bandstand, Joe, myself, George, and Stan, in that order. The house lights came on, and I couldn't see anything because of them. Then a small snap, and it was over! As we were leaving to return to the table, the same voice shouted again across the now rather quiet bar. "Baby, would I like to get into that!"

I turned to Joe and laughed. "Really, he's too much!" I said.

"Go on, you know you love it!" he replied.

"True!" was my only comment.

The following Friday after our return from AC, I attended a Halloween costume party given by Bob Kent. I wore a black turtleneck, tights, mesh hose, a three-quarter length fringe skirt, black shoes with rhinestones, a rhinestone necklace, and four bracelets. George did my hair in pointed bangs with an attachment pony style again and sprayed auburn. I was going alone and took a cab from Dick's apartment. After Bob had taken my coat, I looked for Bill Lopez who was in the kitchen talking with several friends.

"Tommy, you look terrific! Your hair's the end! Is it a wig?" he asked.

"No, just an attachment. George really did a good job, didn't he?"

They all agreed. Then Bill introduced me to several people. After all the introductions, we started taking pictures. I posed for a "pinup" on top of the piano, and also for movies with Bob, Phil, and some others. The evening passed by so quickly that before long the party was over, and one of the guests offered to drive me home.

When I arrived at the house, I couldn't find my keys. I was a bit high and rang Joe's bell. He let me in, and I told him that instead of putting the keys in Dick's mailbox, I must have put them in his. After recalling the account of the evening, I said good-night, went to Dick's, changed, and to bed.

TWELVE

The following week I attended another wedding with my mother. The usual questions were given me. "When are you getting married, Tom?" asked one of my mother's friends. "I'm a grandmother now, you know!"

"Yes, I know, Mrs. Tone, congratulations! But I always say, 'Why buy the cow when you can get the milk free'!"

The shocked woman just smiled and looked at me strangely, and we continued the conversation along other lines, for which I was thankful. I had borrowed one of Marie's mink stoles for Mom to wear, and she looked terrific.

Later, at Joe's, I told him about the wedding. "She was the only woman in mink. Even the bride's mother didn't wear mink. Something similar, but not mink. I felt so good, and I was proud of the way she looked!" I told him.

"Good, I'm glad you had a good time!"

"Good time! I hate weddings at this point. There was a time I used to love them, but I suppose I always pictured myself as the bride and not the groom," I said, smiling at him.

"Figures, pet, it figures," he said.

Thursday, Johnny called from Philly! "I'll be in town Saturday. I'm driving up with some straight friends, so I don't think we'll get to see too much of each other," he told me. "I hope you won't be too angry, but I can't help it!"

"As long as I get to see you, that's all that matters. Call me when you get in. If I'm not at Dick's, try Joe's. I'll be in one of the two places."

I was cleaning Dick's apartment Saturday afternoon when the phone rang. It was Johnny. He told me he was in town and had an audition and would try to stop by when it was over, but that if he couldn't he would meet me at the bar. We chatted, and after he hung up I continued cleaning. At six o'clock, I still hadn't heard from him. Eleven o'clock, and still I hadn't heard. I was worried and upset! I began thinking all sorts of things. *Why should he do this to me? Where is he? Out with someone else right under my nose? I'll murder him when I get my hands on him!* All these things were going through my mind, and the later it became, the worse it was for me.

"Let's go to the bar, Tom," said George. "He'll probably be there. Maybe something came up. Never can tell!"

I knew George was trying to ease my mind, and later as we approached the entrance to the bar, my heart started beating faster. Inside we looked around, but he wasn't there.

"Wrong guess, George! Well, there's nothing I can do! No doubt I'll hear from him tomorrow, but I still would like to know why he hasn't called. It's bugging the hell out of me."

"Like you said, there's nothing you can do but try to enjoy yourself," he said.

I tried, but it was bothering me too much. The evening seemed very long that night, and I was looking forward to the next day, when I hoped I would get the explanation I so needed.

Sunday came and went with no word from Johnny. I was sick with fear and worry! I realized what a fool I must seem to my friends. I took his ring and carefully placed it in the change pocket of my wallet, thinking that I would mail it to him along with a sweater he had left. I wrote a letter, but Joe and George were against my mailing it. Monday it had really gotten to me. *Well, this is it!* I said to myself but nonetheless had to write.

Friday evening he called and told me that he had kept getting a wrong number the week before. I felt it a bit hard to believe after all this time. We talked for awhile, and he told me he would be in town the second week in December. We said our good-byes and promised each other we'd write.

Bob Kent called and invited me to a cocktail party. He said he was showing the pictures from Halloween and also some we had taken with Bill Lopez a few years back. He asked if we were going to the drag and if we needed a lift. I told him that we had ordered a chauffeur-driven limousine to take us but would hold him to the ride back. He agreed, and we would talk further about it at the party.

Thanksgiving dinner was early, as usual. After dinner, I hurried down to Dick's apartment. George set my hair, and we began to dress. After my hair was dry and combed, he added attachments similar to the ones I had worn to the Halloween party and once again sprayed it auburn. He did the same to his own, only his was the ponytail I had worn to the party, whereas mine was in a page-boy style. Then he finished combing out Joe's red wig. Into our sequined bathing suits, mesh hose, and fur stoles we went. I was completely dressed when Joe asked me to pin the bow on his bathing suit.

"I can't now, I've got gloves on, and it's a job to undo them," I told him.

With that he threw off the wig and announced he wasn't going. "You go on without me. I'm so sorry I asked you to remove your gloves!" he said, his voice showing his anger.

"Don't be like that, Joe," I said, almost in tears. "Johnny's here, and he can help you. That's all I meant! He's not as nervous as we are!"

George, not bothered by the whole incident, simply said, "If you're not going, let me have the stole!"

Joe said nothing after that, and I was still upset on the way to the dance in the limousine.

"He's like that, Tom," George said, trying to console me. "It'll all be forgotten in the morning."

"I'm not so sure. He spent hours and weeks helping me,

and then when he asks something simple, what do I go and pull, something stupid like this. I feel terrible!"

"Forget it, Tom," said Dick from his seat in the corner.

As the car approached the entrance to the ballroom, the people once again were lined on both sides. Even in the rain they were there, umbrellas over their heads, shouting and screaming. As George and I left the car, our furs and outfits glittering, there were "ooohs" and "ahhhhs" from the crowd. George made the most of it and posed this way and that, while I practically dashed into the ballroom.

We met a number of people we both knew, had drinks, and made the rounds of the ballroom to see and be seen. About an hour later, George decided to enter the Grand March, and as Dick and I stood waiting for it to start, we looked around, and I saw Joe entering, all smiles.

"Well, I made it after all!" he said.

"Oh, Joe, I'm so happy! You've no idea how perfect this makes the evening!"

Before the dance ended, we decided to separate. Joe and George were to go in Bob Kent's car to a bar on the East Side. I told them I would join them later and would come with Chuck Douglas, into whom I had run earlier and asked to join us.

Half an hour later, Chuck and I left the ballroom. I also had four other boys with me, two on each arm! We walked through the crowd outside and not a word was said, just approval as I stepped into the street and began to walk the long block toward the car that one of the boys had.

The bar was very crowded when we arrived, and I spotted George and Joe at a table near the stage and tried to get their attention. "I have a table reserved," I told the bouncer.

"Sorry, can't go in," he said.

What could we do? Finally, I saw someone I knew and called him over and asked him to tell Joe and George that we couldn't get in and were going home.

"Sure, baby," he said, "and, incidentally, you look great!"

I thanked him and after he gave the message, George came up front and asked the bouncer to let us in, but he said it was too crowded. We decided to go over and visit a friend of ours named Dee, who owned a girls' bar, and left.

We had one drink at Dee's, when I noticed a policeman at the door and became frightened. In drag, I needed a cop like a hole in the head. "George, look, a cop!"

Joe heard this and looked up. "Time for Mother to be home making those Easter eggs. Lovely time, girls, but gotta fly!"

"Hold on a minute!" said Dee. "It's okay!"

"Even so, honey, it's getting late, and we all have to work tomorrow. Thanks for everything, and we'll be in touch," Joe said.

"Okay, Joe—Tommy—George—you all look lovely! And thanks for stopping by!"

After I washed my hair, I went directly to bed. The next day I had it cut to a normal length. *Almost natural now!* I thought to myself as I looked in the mirror. *About time, too. I'd forgotten what the hell it looked like. Not bad, not bad at all! Oops, and look, grey hairs, too! Gettin' old, ain't ya, honey? Oh, well!*

Most everyone who saw my almost normal shade seemed to like it. Even I was getting used to it.

"Does have too many grey hairs," I told George. "But I'm getting it across the center of the forehead and over the side temples. Maybe it might be nice when it's fully grown."

"I can just hear the comments from the dizzy queens when you come into a bar: 'Look, she's got a new color—oops, sorry, my dear. Natural, this time—grey, isn't it?'"

"Very funny, George! But seriously, if it doesn't look good, I'll just dip it again. Not like I used to be, but perhaps a honey blond this time!"

"Do and I'll kill ya." He smiled. "That's my next shade!"

"Oh, *was* it, how nice!"

George gave me a funny look, then we both smiled, and the subject was forgotten.

I heard from Johnny, but his trip was once again canceled. Christmas was coming, and he wanted to try to save money. As much as I cared for him, I was human and needed sex, so I entertained myself with nameless one-nighters, which solved my problems very nicely.

When my Christmas check arrived, I decided to get the shopping over with early. After I had bought several gifts, I went to Joe's to rest before going home. When I arrived, he was on the phone.

"Oh, hi," he said. Then to the phone, "It's Miss Devlin, and she looks like a female Santa Claus. You should see all the packages. Looks like she's robbed half of New York!" He finished his conversation and hung up. We talked for awhile until George came in from work, watched some TV, and then I left for home.

Christmas came and went just as fast! George and I attended midnight Mass in my parents' neighborhood. Then we watched *A Christmas Carol* on the *Late, Late Show*. When it was over, George left and went to his parents' home. He was exhausted because he had worked that day, and naturally it had been one of his busiest!

The following night we went dancing, but the place was so crowded, and we were still tired, so we didn't stay very long. "Why knock ourselves out?" he said. "New Year's is coming, and we can live it up then!"

About fifteen people showed up at Joe's apartment for the 1957–58 party. We went to another party and spent a short time there. Later, in what was now the morning, Johnny Tyler, Fred, Joe, George, and I went to a bar. George wasn't feeling well. He had been to the doctor and received a penicillin shot for the cold he had, so he decided to go home.

After he left, I looked in the back, where a large crowd had gathered. "Hey, Johnny! There's dancing!" I said.

"Dancing!" he echoed. "Let's join them!"

We joined them, not only in watching, but also dancing. Joe left shortly, and the three of us had a few more drinks and the free breakfast that the bar was serving. We were eating when another friend of mine came in who was a terrific dancer, and we began dancing till the wee hours of the morning. Johnny and Fred left, but twinkle toes was still going strong. I arrived home at 8:30 A.M. and fell completely exhausted into bed and slept until 4:00 that afternoon.

In the evening I went to a movie and met a boy from Queens, whom I took to Dick's apartment. He was new to gay life, and it was interesting—for one night! He asked for my number, which I gave him, and said he would call during the week.

Of course, he didn't, and I was thankful, in a way. He was nice, but I really didn't want to get too involved. I still had Johnny, or so I thought, but at this point it was a long-distance romance. I didn't want anyone else around on a permanent basis—not until I was sure about Johnny.

I received a letter from Johnny Parks Saturday afternoon. In it, he explained why he hadn't been in touch. Trouble at home and trying to save money to move to New York permanently were the main reasons he gave. In part, the letter said, "I know you probably won't even want to speak to me again, but I would like us to be friends! I've made a New Year's resolution to write you at least once a week, should you answer this."

I was pleased to see nothing had really changed, and later that evening I called him. We talked for a while, and he said he would come to New York in a few weeks. We spoke a while longer and then promised each other we'd write.

We continued writing for the next few weeks, and in one of his letters he told me there was still trouble and he couldn't get to New York. He asked that I meet him in Philadelphia on March 16. We called and made final arrangements.

I arrived at 1:30, and he was at the station to meet me. We went for something to eat, and since it was a Sunday, no bars were open or liquor sold anywhere because of the blue law in that state. We stopped to watch the St. Patrick's Parade, which was being held a day earlier, and then continued walking as he showed me the city.

Later we went to the bus terminal where he caught his bus home, and I returned to the train station and tried to sleep on the train but couldn't. He was finally coming to New York to live, and we were gong to get a place of our own. *At last!* I thought, *I've finally made it!*

The following weekend, George and I went dancing. When the bar closed, George decided to stay out and cruise, and I continued home. About 6:15 A.M., the phone rang, and George asked me to take him to the hospital. He had dislocated his shoulder getting out of bed. The guy he had picked up had a car, and after I dressed he drove us to the hospital. After spending three hours there, the hospital informed George he would have to have an operation to permanently put his arm in place. At work the following day, he called me and asked to bring some clothes to the hospital. He wasn't having the operation after all. The doctor advised it would be useless until it happened again, which it would if he weren't careful. On my lunch hour I went to the apartment, picked up some clothes, and went to the hospital. I took him downstairs, where his father was waiting to take him home in a cab.

The Bal Fantastique was once again held, and Joe had his outfit planned. I wanted to borrow a wig and go formal for a change, but when I called the boy who was going to lend it to me, he was out of town, and my plans were almost canceled. Joe came up with the idea of my going as a flapper.

"A flapper?" I cried in horror. "You're kidding!"

"Why not? You can borrow the red fringe outfit from Billy. After all, you made it for him, didn't you?" he said.

"Sure, I could borrow it, but I don't want to! Besides, I haven't the things to go with it!"

"We'll arrange something, don't worry!"

"That's what I'm afraid of, you and your bright ideas. You'll look gorgeous, and I'll look like your stooge."

Joe grinned his famous grin and said, "Don't be silly, Sally! You know I don't consider you a stooge!"

"Then why are you hitting me?" I smiled back at him.

Before I realized what had happened, I had borrowed the flapper outfit, and the night of the ball was upon us. Joe, Marie, and I went, and also a girl I used to work with. Marie looked fabulous in her Vampira outfit and had the men after her most of the evening, and she loved it!

THIRTEEN

Bob Knight called a few weeks later and invited George and me to a party in Queens. It wasn't unusual because parties were very common in those days.

George and I arrived late, as always. After saying hello to those we knew and meeting some new people, we proceeded to the kitchen for a drink. I was sitting at the table talking with Bill Lopez and a few others as other guests came in for refills. One by one they left, and as I started out, I noticed my ice was low and returned to get another cube. I was alone, and as I started to leave the kitchen, the bathroom door, which was diagonally opposite the kitchen, opened. Standing in its doorway with a forced smile was Johnny Parks. I was both shocked and surprised to see him. I wondered who had arranged it. I smiled and said, "What are you doing here? Was this prearranged, or what?"

He just shrugged his shoulders and said nothing. Finally, he said, "No, Tommy, it wasn't arranged. I'm going into the army next Tuesday, and I don't think it's fair for you to wait two years. I'm up here on my last fling!"

I couldn't fully grasp what he was saying at first and went into the kitchen and sat down at the table. "Why like this, Johnny?"

"I figured it was the best way, what with my parents and everything. I had written you a letter explaining everything. Of all the parties we have to run into each other here," he said.

"Johnny, these people are close friends of mine. I have

more of a right here than you! Incidentally, who are you here with?" I asked.

"Some friends from the dance school," he replied.

"Oh, I see!"

"I'd better get back. I'll come over tomorrow and explain! If not, I'll call you anyway."

"All right, Johnny, if that's the way you want it!"

Without another word, he left and went to the playroom where the others were dancing. Still shaken about the whole incident, I rose and again started to leave, as Bill Lopez came in.

"Tommy, I'm so sorry about what's happened! When they told me who he was, I nearly died!"

"It's okay, Bill, really it is!"

"Don't kid me, honey, I know you're upset to no end, and what I have to tell you isn't going to make it any easier. Tommy, please don't think I'm a bitch, but you've got to know."

"Know what, Bill? That Johnny doesn't love me? That he's made a complete fool out of me in front of all my friends? I know it, Bill. Trouble is, I'm in love with him!"

I looked at Bill, who had tears swelling in his eyes. "Oh, Tommy," he continued, "you don't know the half of it!"

"You mean there's more? What else can there be?"

"Well, here it comes! Prepare yourself, baby, it's a whopper! You know that boy Johnny's with, Rudy?" he asked.

"I just met him. Why?"

"Well, from what I understand, they've been going together for a month and a half."

His words stung as though I had been hit with a blunt instrument.

"He's been lying to you, Tom, all the time. I'm so sorry, baby! I'd have given anything not to have been the one to tell you this, but you had to know!" he said softly.

"Who else knows?" I asked, knowing the answer.

"Everyone!"

My heart sank as he told me, and I turned to face the wall so he wouldn't see the tears that had started.

"Go ahead, cry, if you think it will do any good. Cry and get it out of your system. Don't be ashamed!"

"Oh, Bill, I *am* ashamed; I can't believe it. It's like something you hear or read about but never think it can happen to you."

"But it has, Tommy, and I know you. For awhile you'll be upset, but you always manage to land on you feet. You always do!"

Composing myself a bit, I turned to Bill. "Thanks, Bill. Thanks for being the one to tell me. I'm glad it was you—and I don't think you're a bitch. I think you're the greatest. I love you! Now, if you'll excuse me, there's a slight score I have to settle."

"Where are you going?" he asked.

I gave him a weak smile and left the kitchen and walked steadily toward the playroom. Slipping off the wedding band Johnny had given me, I went directly to where he and Rudy were seated. My voice was low but loud enough for others nearby to hear, among them Bill, whom I saw from the corner of my eye standing in the doorway.

"I understand you and Rudy have been going together for a month and a half! I'm sure he'll have more use for this than I!" I gently slipped the ring into Johnny's shirt pocket, turned, and left the room. As I was going to the kitchen, I passed Bill and smiled.

"Orchids to you, Miss Devlin! You handled the situation beautifully, as I knew you would. If it were me, I'd have scratched his eyes out!"

I got another drink and joined George in the living room. He had heard the scene I just had had.

"What are you doing here?"

"Long story, Jennie! I'm among the single women again! I

could just kill him for the embarrassment he's caused me tonight. Of all parties, why did it have to be here, with everyone I know!"

"Probably just as well. If he's like that, it's better you found out now than after you moved in together."

Of course, George was right. But it wasn't that easy to forget.

"I know it'll be weeks before you'll be able to go home with anyone else and feel relaxed with them."

I tried my best to have a good time, but my mind was constantly on Johnny. Every once in awhile I'd casually look in his direction, but he avoided my eyes. Bill and I danced a good part of the evening, and when we did, many others left the floor to watch.

After one strenuous dance, I decided to freshen up and headed for the bathroom. The door was locked, so I waited. A few minutes later it opened, and Johnny started out. I looked around and pushed him back in, saying, "I want to talk to you!" I locked the door and turned to face him. "Now, what the hell is this all about? Why have you lied to me?"

"I don't know. Tom, I'm so terribly mixed-up. I've even been seeing a shrink."

"A likely story! This guy you're with, are you in love with him?"

"Very much!"

"Well, I guess that's that, isn't it? I could hate you, but I don't! One can't help the way the heart feels. I'm just a bit disappointed in you for not being honest with yourself and me."

"I wanted to, Tom, but I knew how you felt."

"And knowing this you led me on and lied to me? Oh, Johnny, I'd have more respect for you if you only came and told me to my face that you didn't care for me, rather than have to find out this way."

"I didn't have the courage to face you after awhile. When I

heard you were here, I ran in here to try to muster up the courage to face you."

"It's no use, Johnny! I probably still love you, but I could never trust you again, and when trust is gone, how much love can be left? Right now, I'm confused and mixed-up myself. I say I love you, but at this point, I really don't know. Not now, anyway!"

"I'd better go! They're probably wondering what we're doing in here!"

"Let them wonder. Don't I deserve this much consideration?"

"Of course!"

Simultaneously, we kissed, then broke our embrace. I saw there were tears in his eyes, and, of course, there were in mine.

"Tommy, I don't want it to end like this. I'm so sorry!"

"So am I! I know it's over but try to come over tomorrow or call."

"I'll try!" he said and left the bathroom.

I finished my toilet and went to the kitchen for another drink. Bill was there and I said, "Might as well get loaded!"

"Don't think about it, Tom. It's better to try and forget it as quickly as possible. Go out and get someone who can do something for you. Forget these kids. They only bring you down. Go after money, baby, that's all that really matters!"

"I know, but I can't. I just can't!"

"Sure, you can. Give yourself a chance! Once you've done it, it isn't so bad!" he said.

I smiled and filled my glass.

"Tom, why not come to the Island some weekend. Chuck [his present new lover] and I have a house this year, and, you know how much I want to really show you the Island. I know you've been there, but we've never been there together. It'll be a ball, baby!"

"Okay, I'll try. No promises, mind you, but I'll try!"

"You always say that! What have you against the place?"

"Nothing really, Bill. I'm just not that big for the beach anymore. You know that!"

"There are other things besides the beach. You'll meet a lot of people; we know half the Island. Think about it, okay?"

We left and joined the others, and I tried my best to enjoy myself. I looked and saw Johnny and his friends leaving. "Guess I won out after all; they're leaving," I said to George.

He looked at me as if to say, "You're nuts, Tommy, completely, absolutely, crazy," but he just nodded.

Dick wasn't home when I arrived at the apartment, and I was glad. I wanted to be alone. After I got into bed, I started thinking about the evening, and the tears came freely. *Oh, Johnny! I'm such a fool, but I do love you!* I said to myself and cried for some time until sleep won the battle.

The following evening after dinner, George, Jerry, and I went to a movie. Each started for a separate theater to cruise and promised to meet at eleven o'clock if we hadn't met anyone. At eleven, only Jerry and I showed up.

"Figures, doesn't it?" I smiled on greeting him. "Guess George met someone. Where do you want to go?" I asked.

"Doesn't matter. They're all the same!" he answered.

I agreed. We decided to go to the nearest bar, and after we got our drinks, Jerry met a friend and started talking with him. I went over and stood near a wall, looking as if I were part of the fixtures.

"Hi! Seen Sal lately?" asked a voice to my left.

I turned, and it was a friend of Sal's whom I had met a few weeks earlier when I had run into Sal in a bar. I couldn't remember his name and said, "No, I haven't! That stinker was supposed to call, but you know Sal. His intentions are good, but for some strange reason he never thinks of calling!"

"I know! But we've been busy rehearsing almost nightly,

and by the time it's over, it's too late to call anyone, so don't be too hard on him!" he said, smiling.

"Well, under the circumstances I guess I can't! Just tell him I said hello when you see him, and if he does get a chance, have him call me, okay?"

"Okay, I will!"

We talked for some time, and then he excused himself and went to the back of the bar. Jerry, came over and asked me who he was, and I told him he was Sal's partner, but that I'd forgotten his name. About then he came back with a drink, and we continued our conversation.

"So how have you been?" he asked.

"Fine!" I replied, then, "Incidentally, I'm a bit embarrassed! I can't recall your name!"

"That's okay, I've forgotten yours, too. Mine's Nicky."

"Nicky!" I repeated. "Of course!" I told him mine and introduced him to Jerry. We all talked for a while longer, and then Jerry said he was leaving.

About 1:00 A.M. Nicky and I left the bar. "At least I have company going home," I said.

We exchanged phone numbers, and he asked me to call. We arranged that I call the following night about 6:30, which I did, and we talked for a few minutes. He told me he was expecting a call from Sal, that they were having trouble with their group, and that if he got out of rehearsals early enough he would call me.

I went to Joe's later and watched TV with him till about eleven, when I decided to call it a night. I was talking with Stan on our phone when Joe knocked on my door.

"Nicky's in a phone booth and wants you to call him," he said, handing me a slip of paper. I had given Nicky both numbers, as I did with most people because of the fact I spent so much time at Joe's.

I told Stan I'd call him back and hung up and dialed the number Joe had given me.

"Hi!" he said. "I'm free! Where can I meet you?"

"Oh, hon, it's late, and I'm ready for bed," I answered.

"Oh, come on Tom, just one drink!" he urged.

"Force me!"

"Consider yourself forced! Say, in half an hour in the Village at the Colony?" he suggested.

"A half hour it is!"

I hung up, dialed Stan again, and told him I had a date and couldn't talk too long. We chatted for a few minutes then hung up, and I dressed. Twenty minutes later I was in the bar. We sat and talked for an hour and a half before I realized how late it was getting and had to leave.

"It was nice seeing you again, Tom. I really do enjoy your company!" he said as we were leaving the bar.

"And I yours, Nicky. You're so easy to talk with, it's a pleasure."

We took the train together, and when my stop came, I said, "Well, here's my stop! Call me, will you?"

"I will, and, Tommy, thanks for a pleasant evening!"

"Nicky, as I said before, it's my pleasure!" We smiled at each other as the train left the station. I was very tired when I reached the apartment and went directly to bed.

In the days that followed, we saw a lot of each other, all this unknown to Sal.

"Even though there's nothing between us, I just don't want him to know," he explained one evening.

"I understand! Tell him I'm doing secretarial work for you."

"Yeah! That's a good idea! Would you?"

"Would I what?" I asked, not knowing what he was talking about.

"Help with the secretarial end of things. You've a good head for business correspondence, and I could use someone. I can't afford to pay you, but—"

"Nicky , I'd love to help, and I don't expect to be paid. I like helping people; you know that," I replied.

So it was settled that I'd help out. A few days later he told me he and Sal were having pictures taken for promotion work on the record they hoped to record. I called a place that rented evening clothes and set up an appointment for them and arranged to meet Nicky in a restaurant. Sal was to join us later. When he arrived he was surprised to see me, especially since I was with Nicky.

"Hi!" he said. "For Pete's sake, where did you come from?"

"I just ran into Tommy and asked him to have coffee with me. I told him you were coming!" said Nicky. This all had been prearranged between us.

After their fitting was finished, we took the subway downtown and planned on meeting later that evening. Nicky said he had to go home and Sal didn't have any plans until we met later, so I asked him to come to the apartment while I changed.

When we got there, Dick was shaving, and Joe was reading. As we entered, Joe looked up and said, "Hi, Sal! Where's the towel and shirt you owe us?" I had completely forgotten he had borrowed the towel when we had gone to the beach one day and the shirt belonged to Tim. Sal just smiled and said hello but ignored the question. I changed as quickly as possible, and we left to have dinner.

When dinner was over, I asked Sal to return to the apartment while I shaved and got ready for the evening. He told me he'd rather not, and that I could do all that at his place. I knew why he didn't want to go back, and he waited downstairs while I went up and got the things I needed. At his apartment, after I had showered and shaved, we sat down and had a few drinks. There was still time before we were to meet Nicky.

"Nice place, Sal, but isn't it a bit expensive for you?" I inquired.

"Yes, but I like it!"

"So, what's new? Who is it this week?" I asked, smiling.

"This week?" he said. "I'll have you know I've been going with the same person for almost a year now!"

"Well, la-de-dah! What do you want, a medal?"

"No, but I think it's terrific!" he said.

"I do, too, baby. The best, and I mean that! Well, it's getting late. We'd better get started if we're to meet Nicky," I suggested.

"He's always late. Don't worry."

I wanted to tell him he was never late with me but kept my mouth shut.

In the weeks that followed little came of their record, and I did even less in the way of secretarial work. The end result was that they decided to give up the idea of show business careers and broke up the group. Nicky and I saw a great deal of one another during this period, although there was never anything sexual or serious in our relationship. We'd meet for an occasional movie or for drinks but nothing more. Then, as quickly as it had started, the phone calls became fewer on both our parts, and we saw one another only rarely.

FOURTEEN

The music from the radio faded as I went into the kitchen. From the cabinet above the sink, I took a small bottle labeled CREAM BEIGE—LIQUID MAKEUP, walked to the mirror, and began applying it. After I had finished, I looked in the mirror and was pleased with the results. It seemed to say, "Hope it's not all in vain." *Most likely it will be,* I said to myself. *I seem to have the luck of the Irish lately—all bad.* I was putting on a sweater when the phone rang. I had made arrangements to meet Johnny Taylor and Bill Bushe later and wondered who was calling or who had changed his mind. I turned the radio down low and answered the phone. It was Johnny!

"Hi, what's up? Aren't you coming?" I asked.

"Don't worry, I'll be there! Just wanted to let you know I'll be a little late. I have something to take care of here at the last minute before I leave," he said.

"Okay, I'll call Bill and tell him. What time will you be here?"

"About eleven. Is that okay?"

"Sure! I don't want to go out too early, anyway. Spend too much money that way!"

We hung up, and I called Bill and told him Johnny would be late and I would call him when he got here.

After my call to Bill, I went into the living room, turned the radio up again and lit a cigarette. I picked up a magazine as the radio played. I looked into space and thought, *The memories that song has. It was playing the night Johnny Parks and I met! Was it only several months age? Seems longer,* I said to myself. I continued reading for some time. Later, I heard a knock on the door. When I answered it, Johnny Tyler was standing there, one hand on his hip, and the other on the side of the door.

"Your bell doesn't work. I've been ringing for about five minutes. Finally I rang Joe's. He's gonna be wondering who it is," he said.

"Don't worry. We'll go up before we leave and say good night to the doll and tell her my bell isn't working. Make yourself a drink while I call Bill."

After calling Bill we sat and talked for a while, went up to Joe's to say hello, and then left to pick Bill up. We made the rounds of the bars, and later after Bill went home, Johnny, and I went to a restaurant to which I had been before and wanted him to see.

"You won't believe this place, Johnny," I told him in the car as we drove uptown. "There's all kinds, all shapes, mostly the effeminate, but it's a gas!"

After he parked the car we entered the restaurant. I sat at a table to hold it while he went for coffee. As I was waiting, I heard pieces of conversations.

"Hi, Mae, how ya been? Your hair's the end! When did ya dip it?"

"There's a gorgeous piece of trade that hangs out near my sister's house, and he's the living end. Last night I was walking along minding my own business, when—oh, hi, sweetie—"

As I listened to these conversations, I wondered how they, managed to keep jobs what with bleached hair, long nails, and whatnot. As I was thinking this, Johnny came with the coffee.

"This place is too much," he said as he sat down. "Fred wouldn't believe it!"

We sat and talked for some time. We mentioned my breakup with Johnny Parks, our coming vacation together, and Roger's sending me an airline ticket to come to Washington so I wouldn't have any excuse for not going.

"I'm looking forward to the Washington weekend. I just hope I'll have a good time," I finally said.

"I'm sure you will, and tell Roger I love him for doing this for you. He must be a wonderful person to think so much of you," he said.

"He is, Johnny. One of the nicest I've met in a long time. Actually, in a way, you two are very much alike. Not physically, of course, but both wonderful people whom I love and admire very much. You know, I met him when I was working in the bar a few years back."

"Yes, I remember you telling me about him. And it's easy being nice when you have a friend as sweet and wonderful as you, Tommy!" he answered.

I thanked him, and shortly we left the restaurant. We were to call during the week to make plans for the coming weekend, as we had been doing since we first met.

The following Friday I met an older man who told me he was a photographer. I wasn't interested in him, but he was friendly. "Have you ever thought of modeling?" he asked after introducing himself.

"No!" I replied.

"I'm sure you could do sportswear. Why not try some time?" he continued.

"That's easier said than done!"

"No, it isn't! Look, I'd like to see some pictures of you, and that way I'll be able to tell if you're photogenic or not."

I wondered what kind of a kook I had met this time, but what the hell, what did I have to lose? I certainly wouldn't go to bed with this guy, and I made that quite clear, telling him I had a lover. He told me his name was Al, and our conversation drifted from one subject to another. He seemed harmless enough, although he was ruining my cruising. I didn't want to be rude or say anything, so we continued talking until the bar closed. We had coffee, and he still wanted to see some pictures of me. After coffee we went to the apartment, and I showed him my album. After seeing several pictures, he told me I definitely could and should model.

"Your measurements are perfect for your height. Just have to gain two inches on your chest to have a completely perfect physical structure," he told me. Naturally, hearing this I was pleased, and since he hadn't made any sexual advances, I thought perhaps he might be on the level. We talked until 7:00 A.M., when he left. Before he did, he asked me to call him to make a date so he could take some pictures of me. I agreed.

Several days later, after taking pictures at Al's apartment, we had dinner. Every thing seemed to go very well, and again he made no sexual advances, which pleased me. After dinner, I told him I had to get back because I was meeting my "lover" and didn't want to be late. We made another date to take more pictures the following weekend, and I left.

When I arrived the following weekend, he introduced me to another boy and told me we were going to pose together. This time we were to pose nude. I started to tell him I didn't pose like that, but he said they weren't going to be "dirty" pictures. I then agreed, undressed, and posed with the young man whose name was Richard. The poses were similar to those I had seen in muscle magazines, only they had clothes on, and we didn't.

When the session was over, Richard and I left. Al's apartment was on the second floor, and rather than wait for the elevator, we took the staircase. On the staircase, Richard stopped and grabbed me. After he had orally relieved me, we left and went our separate ways. I never saw him again.

I kept asking Al to see the pictures he had taken, but he always made some excuse. They were either being printed or he had to go out that night. It got to a point where I actually thought he didn't have film in the camera and was getting off on seeing people naked. I mentioned this to a few friends, and they agreed. After that, I decided it was better to forget about "modeling," but most of all, Al.

I called Johnny Tyler one evening shortly before our trip to the Cape, and we talked about it at length.

"I'm so excited about the trip, Tom. I can hardly wait."

"Me too!" I told him. "You'd think it was my first plane trip or my first time to the Cape. Actually, it's been so long I hardly remember what it's like. I'm sure you're going to like it, though."

"I'm sure I will, Tom."

The following Friday I was off to Washington. I arrived at the airline terminal at 6:45 P.M. and waited for my flight announcement. At 6:55, the flight was announced as last call, so I put out my cigarette and rushed through the gate, had my ticket taken, and boarded the plane. *Last call, indeed,* I thought, looking around the almost empty plane. *I could have broken my neck rushing like this.* I took a window seat and was looking out the window as more passengers boarded, when I heard a man ask me if the seat next to me was taken. I told him no, and he sat down and began to read a newspaper. The plane finally began to taxi down the runway at 7:15 and then stood waiting for clearance. At 7:25 the pilot announced there was going to be a slight delay in taking off and arriving in Washington due to the rain conditions. *Swell,* I thought. *Roger and Bill [his lover of a few years] will be waiting for hours at this rate..*

Finally, the plane started down the runway, and we were up in the air in a matter of minutes. The man next to me took out a cigar as soon as the NO SMOKING sign went off, lit it, and began puffing away and reading his paper. I hate cigar smoke, but knew I had to put up with it for the next hour. The trip was smooth, and we flew above the clouds. The sun was shining beautifully, and it seemed hard to believe that down below the earth lay in fog and mist.

When dinner was served, the flight attendant brought me

my tray, which consisted of meat. As it was Friday, I couldn't eat it and asked if she had anything else.

"Only swordfish," she said with a beautiful smile.

"No, thanks, don't like seafood, either!" I replied.

"I'm sorry, sir," she said, "but perhaps you could at least eat the vegetables."

I did and also finished my little strawberry shortcake and coffee. Relaxed, I lit a cigarette and looked at my watch. *Eight-thirty! Should be there soon,* I thought to myself.

Ten minutes later we arrived at the Washington airport. I saw Roger and Bill, whom I hadn't met yet, waiting for me near the exit gate as the plane's engines came to a halt. As I was seated near the front of the plane, I was one of the first passengers to leave and greeted them.

"I thought I'd never get here! The plane was held up in New York because of the weather."

"Just as well," said Roger. "We just got here ourselves. Got held up with Bill's dad talking and didn't realize the time, so it worked out best all around, didn't it?"

He then introduced me to Bill, whom I liked immediately.

After getting my luggage, we walked to the car and drove to Roger's house. Along the way he pointed out what he thought would be of interest to me, as this was my first trip to D.C.

"That's the White House, Tom. I know a trip to Washington isn't complete without seeing it, so there it is!"

"Hummm, looks just like all the pictures I've seen. Wonder why everything just looks like pictures you've seen. Sounds crazy, doesn't it?" I laughed.

We arrived an hour later at the house, and Roger showed me to the guest room.

"This is my folks' place. They're in Canada for the summer, and I'm going to have my party here Sunday. They said it was okay as long as we clean up afterwards," he said.

"It's a lovely house, Roger, really lovely, and so's this room!"

He gave me a peck on the cheek and asked me if I'd like a sandwich, which I said I would and told him of the incident on the plane. After I showered, I joined them in the kitchen, and we had sandwiches and coffee. Later we had a few beers. About 11:00 the phone rang, and Roger answered it. After he hung up, he said it was a friend of his named Lee who was at the bus terminal, and he was going to pick him up and asked if I'd like to go for the ride. I told him I would. We stopped for cigarettes after picking Lee up and then returned to the house. Roger said another friend named Marve who was in the service was also due to arrive at any minute. About 1:00 A.M. I told them I was beat and was going to bed if they didn't have any objections.

"I'll have to meet him in the morning, but I'm really tired. We were very busy at work today."

"Okay, good night Tom, sleep well," they all said, and I went upstairs and got into bed. Later, I turned my head toward the sound of voices. "Tom, this is Marve! Marve, Tom. You two are sleeping together, if you don't mind!"

"Hi!" he said.

"Hi," I replied, then added, "Nice way to meet someone, isn't it? In bed, I mean. It *is* different!" We all laughed, and I fell asleep almost before Roger closed the door.

Rog (Roger) called me for breakfast, and I saw I was alone in the room with him.

"Where is everyone?" I asked.

"Having breakfast, sleepyhead!" he replied, smiling.

"Am I the last to get up?"

"Oh, Rog, why didn't you wake me sooner? I feel terrible!"

"No matter, nothing to do anyway. We're going to the cabin later, so take your time dressing and bring a bathing suit in case we go swimming when we get there," he said, leaving the room.

"Will do!"

With breakfast over and the dishes done, we got in the car for the ride to Chesapeake Bay, where they had a cabin. It was a long ride, but I enjoyed it. The scenery was beautiful, and the sun tried desperately to shine. An hour later we arrived. I never saw anything so peaceful looking. The cabin was on a cliff overlooking the bay. Made of chestnut, it was clean and modern with both an upstairs and downstairs. After the tour we had drinks and sandwiches. The drinks began to affect me for some strange reason, probably Roger's heavy hand with the liquor. I began to feel quite mellow.

Later in the afternoon we searched the beach for driftwood, which I had mentioned I would like to have, and came across a small piece. It wasn't exactly what I wanted, but it would have to do. We returned to the cabin and while Marve and I were downstairs, we began kissing. The liquor we had consumed helped, but we decided to go upstairs because it didn't look right. When we arrived upstairs, no one was around. I thought perhaps Roger and the others had gone for a drive, and Marve and I had another drink. We sat on the sofa and started making love again. We climaxed only minutes before we heard a car stop outside the cabin.

"We needed some bread and decided to take a drive," Rog said, smiling, handing us each an ice-cream cone. I knew immediately why they had left but said nothing.

Next day on the way back to Washington, I fell asleep as the rain slashed against the car windows.

The party on Sunday was a small affair and I was introduced to Rog's friends, most of whom had lovers, so cruising was out. I was still on vacation, and on Monday Roger and I drove to Friendship Airport to see the new jet that was on display. After our return, I packed, had dinner, and he drove me to the airport. The plane was held up again and didn't take off until ten o'clock, one and a half hours late.

After I settled down in my seat, I looked around. The plane was half empty, and I tried to read but couldn't. I was thinking of the quiet and relaxed time I had, and how nice it would be to spend it there with someone I cared for—some time! When we reached La Guardia, I took a cab to the apartment, unpacked, and went to bed.

In August, Johnny Tyler and I boarded the plane for our trip to the Cape. It was Johnny's first time on a plane, and he was very nervous. The ride was considerably smooth until we approached the Boston airport, when it started shaking and moving from side to side. Johnny was very upset, and I kept talking about anything to take his mind off the landing. I was used to it! Seasoned traveler that I was now, after three or four flights, it didn't bother me. After we landed, he seemed to feel more at ease.

The Cape had changed! More shopping areas had opened, and the town itself had become very commercial. Bill Bushe and a friend of his had also decided to go that week and were staying at another guest house.

Johnny was extremely hairy, and when Bill saw him on the beach, he asked, "And how's your fur jacket, Johnny?"

He smiled and took it in stride, and we joked about it for some time. "Volare" was one of the popular songs, and whenever it played on the radio, Bill would start singing along, substituting his own lyrics, which were very funny and had everyone in stitches. Four days after we had gotten there, I noticed that Johnny, was acting strangely.

"What's wrong? Aren't you having a good time?" I asked him one morning before leaving for the beach.

"Oh, it's not that. I'm having a wonderful time, but I miss Fred."

"I thought so. But let's face it, you're on vacation, so stop thinking about it—you'll make me feel bad."

"I'm sorry, Tom, but I can't lie to you. I'm going home this afternoon! I've called Fred and told him to meet the plane. I'm leaving on the two-o'clock flight."

I was disappointed but said, "Well, if you'd feel better, then go! I understand. Don't give it another thought."

We said our good-byes, and I left for the beach to join Bill and the others.

"Where's Johnny?" Bill asked when I arrived.

"Misses his lover and is going home this afternoon," I told them.

We made small jokes about it for a while. At 2:30, I looked at the sky in time to see a little plane take off. I knew he was on it. *Bye, John, have fun. I'll miss you!* I said to myself, and out loud, "Well, there he goes!"

"Well, at least he's got a nice day for flying," said Bill.

"Yes, he certainly has."

The remainder of the week was wonderful. The weather was perfect and Bill and I met a number of people.

"I thought you and that dark-haired boy were lovers!" said a man I was talking with one night in the bar.

"No, just friends, but everyone always thinks we are!"

"Well, the contrast is good—he's dark, and you're light!"

A few months later I returned to the Cape—this time alone. One evening, as I was leaving the bar, I was pulled to the side by another dark-haired, very handsome young man whom I had seen earlier that day at The Moors.

"Leaving so soon?" he asked.

"Yes, I'm tired, and I'm going home!" I replied.

"Would you like to go with me?" he asked.

"Yes, I would very much."

I was surprised at his forwardness and my own as well and felt very flattered. We walked through town and down a long, dark, lonely road to his hotel. His name was Ray, and he was quite drunk, and I was a big high myself. When we arrived at his hotel, we went to bed immediately.

"I still think you're beautiful, and I say that now that I'm sober. I must have been a mess last night! I'm sorry," Ray said the following morning after we got up.

"Don't be! You behaved very well, and I think you're crazy if you think I'm beautiful. I've never been told that before. It's very flattering!" I answered.

"Well, you are! Your hair is beautiful, you carry yourself well, you're friendly, and so many little things that add up to making a person beautiful. You know you're the only platinum blond in town!"

"Am I? I wasn't aware of it," I lied, knowing I hadn't seen anyone with hair as light as mine.

"Honey, , you'd stand out in any crowd!"

I blushed and thanked him. After breakfast, we exchanged addresses, and since he was leaving that afternoon, we said our farewells and promised to keep in touch.

Sunday came, and I packed for the trip home. Two boys I had met during the week drove me to the airport.

"Hate to see you leave, Tom! We've enjoyed meeting and being with you. You must come and visit us in Pittsburgh some time!"

"I'd love to, and thanks for everything—you've both been wonderful! Look, don't bother waiting for the plane to leave, it's a beautiful day, so get back to the beach. Besides, I hate good-byes!"

"Okay, but keep in touch!" they said and left.

After I checked in, I sat down to await the plane since I was early. *Gee, there are nice people!* I thought, lighting a cigarette.

I thought of many things while waiting there, and soon I'd be home, and tomorrow I'd be in Washington with Roger and Bill. How I was looking forward to seeing them again.

The bus ride the following day was something I could have done without—long, tiring, and boring! Roger and Bill met me at the terminal, and we drove directly to the cabin. When we arrived, we had something to eat and then went to bed.

All week they let me sleep late, and on nice days we would drive down to the beach. The week was quiet and peaceful, and I felt marvelous.

One evening we decided to go to an outdoor movie. When we arrived, the sun still hadn't set completely and we were the first people there, so we decided to walk a bit. I was wearing walking shorts, and as we stood talking, a hornet stung me on the right thigh, and I let out a scream. Rog told me to stand still and immediately put his mouth over where I had been stung and sucked out the poison. We then drove back to the cabin, where he put some ointment on it. It was black and blue for days, but there wasn't any pain. Never did see a movie that night.

"It's wonderful being here, Rog," I said one afternoon. "You two couldn't be more perfect hosts had you rehearsed!" I continued.

"We did!" he said with a big smile. "But to tell the truth, we love having you and wish you could come down here to live. You could be happy, I know!"

"Perhaps, Rog, but I'm too confused now, and, well, just give me time!"

My week seemed to fly by, and once again it was time to return home. The bus ride this time was made even more uncomfortable because an extremely heavyset woman sat in the seat next to me and had a good portion of her body on my seat as well. So, for almost six hours I had to put up with it. *Never again by bus!* I thought.

I returned to work the next day, rested and beautifully tanned—for the first time in my life.

In September, Allison Conley, a friend of Joe Davidson's and myself whom we had known for some time, took a furnished apartment on West Fifteenth Street. It was small, dirty, and expensive, but it was a place. I didn't attend the annual drag as the years before. Instead, I stayed at my parents' longer than usual so I would purposely miss it. Was the desire fading? I had hoped so!

The season for parties was now in full swing, and I attended every one to which I was asked. At Bob Kent's Christmas party, I became very high and told three people I would go with them, but only went with one. In the beginning of December, Allison and I had had the place on Fifteenth Street and started looking around for something better. Because there was a newspaper strike, we had to walk up and down different blocks looking for rental signs.

One evening after work, I started making my rounds in a heavy snowstorm. I was walking up West Seventy-fifth Street when I spotted a sign and inquired about the apartment. It was large, furnished, one flight up in the rear of the building, very clean, and very nice. I told the super I would leave a deposit and wanted my roommate to see it. After Allison saw it, we decided it was much better than what we had, and so we moved in that weekend. We had a third roommate, a friend of mine named Joe, who I had known for some time. However, Joe was hardly home, so Allison and I had the place to ourselves most of the time.

New Year's Eve 1958–59, we gave another bottle party. Because the apartment had a large living room, we invited many people. Most everyone showed up. The noise was handled very well, and we didn't have any complaints. Later I decided to bring what was left of our party to another one to which I had been invited. I excused myself to go out and call the host from a corner phone since our phone hadn't been installed yet. As I was going down the steps of the stoop, the heel of my shoe somehow got caught in the cuff of my trousers, and I slipped and fell, landing on my right hand, slightly injuring three fingers but not seriously. After the call I returned to the apartment and put a bandage on my hand, and via four cabs took my party downtown. We stayed until 6:00 A.M. at which time, tired and quite drunk, I left and took a cab home.

FIFTEEN

New Year's day of 1959 was spent drinking Bloody Marys, after which George, Allison, and I went to Bill Bushe's for cocktails. As we were leaving, the rain that had started earlier was coming down very heavily, but we decided to go dancing.

Allison and I were standing, talking and drinking, when someone asked George to dance. I started talking with a waiter I knew. A dark-haired boy in a red sweater entered and proceeded directly to the waiter and began talking with him. Looking over at me, he smiled and said, "Hi! How are you?"

"Fine, thank you. And you?"

The young man and the waiter continued their conversation. From time to time he would look over at me, and naturally I was looking back. Finally, I said, "I know we've met before, but I can't think of where. Let's dance and think about it."

He agreed and after formal introductions had been made (his name was Chuck), we danced for some time, holding one another tightly. At one point he turned to me and said, "You know something? We've never met before, but I have seen you!"

"I know! And isn't it a wonderful way to meet?"

After that first night, we saw each other about once or twice a week. We felt something for each other, but it wasn't enough—on Chuck's part! We began seeing less of each other, and one evening I gave a small party and invited him and his roommate. We argued because I had seen him with someone else during the week. After we both calmed down, we decided it was best not to see one another for awhile and let our relationship cool a bit. I agreed, even though I did like him.

The next night I attended a birthday party with George in the Village. I knew most of the people and drank heavily, trying to forget Chuck. Later we went to a bar. Dancing bars were very popular, as I said before, and we loved them. It was crowded, and I ran into a friend of mine named Shelly, who was in the army, and we began dancing. He was a good dancer, and we danced most of the evening.

I spotted Chuck and asked him to dance. When it was over and we were saying good-bye, Chuck said, "Yes, you'd better go back to your marine, he's waiting for you!"

"Army, dear! And he's just a friend," I snapped back.

"Oh yeah, sure!"

"Well, he is, and even if he weren't, would it matter to you?"

I smiled and left him standing on the dance floor and returned to the crowd. I looked over and saw him looking at me with a sad expression. One by one the others left, and I was almost alone, Chuck having left as well. At 2:30, tired and hungry, I left the bar—alone!

A few weeks later, we moved to the ground-floor apartment, which was larger and a bit more expensive but much nicer. George's birthday was coming up, and we sent out invitations, verbal ones given in the bars and by phone. Johnny Parks and I had been corresponding from time to time, and I asked him as well. I was anxious to see him. After all, it had been nine months since that incident at Bob's, and although by this time it was a forgotten issue, I still had to see him—just to be sure!

By 10:15 the evening of the party several guests had arrived. At one point when our doorbell rang, I answered it and was greeted by a smiling Johnny. Behind him were Millie and George (I had worked with them many years before). I showed

Johnny where to change and unpack, and we stood talking for a few minutes.

"You look wonderful Johnny. I'm glad you could make it!"

"So am I, and you look wonderful, too!"

"Thanks! Make yourself at home, shower if you wish, everything's here. I've got to get back to my guests!"

The party turned out to be a huge success, and everyone seemed to be enjoying themselves, and in doing so caused a great deal of noise, which resulted in the arrival of the police. When they arrived, only four people were in the apartment, and they just told us to keep the noise down. After the last guest had left, Johnny and I said good night and went to our separate beds.

The following morning after breakfast, Allison, Johnny, and I talked and had a few drinks. George came over to help clean up the apartment, but the conversation was interesting and the drinks better, so little was done to clean up the mess of the previous night. A few hours later, Allison and George left for a movie, and Johnny and I talked of old times. When it was time for him to leave to get his bus, I went to the terminal with him.

"I'll write soon," he said. "And thanks for a great weekend. I had a wonderful time—I always do with you!"

"Thanks, and I'll be expecting that letter!" I replied.

He smiled and slowly walked through the gate to his waiting bus. After the bus pulled out, I left and walked toward the subway. *You've changed, Johnny!* I thought to myself. *It can never be the same again. Just as well!* I took the train back to the apartment to clean it before Allison returned from the movie.

Several weeks later, Allison and I had a misunderstanding, which resulted in our mutual desire to move. Joe had since given up his interest in the apartment, and it was getting to be a bit of an expense on the both of us, anyway. We had a week to move because our rent was due weekly. I had thought of moving home, although I really didn't want to. The Sunday before we were scheduled to move, I was at home listening to records and wondering what I was going to do, when the doorbell rang. I was surprised to see Johnny Parks with three other boys. To my continued surprise, they were boys I had met several weeks ago in a bar.

"I'm so surprised and happy you know these kids, Johnny," I said. "They're very nice!"

"Yes," he answered, "and Cecil is the boy I wrote you about that I met on the bus and lives in my hometown. Isn't that something?"

We had coffee, talked, and danced for awhile. Later at the front door, as they were leaving, Cecil turned to me and said, "Look, if you're stuck for a place, you're more than welcome to stay with me. I have a small place on West Eighty-ninth Street I only use on weekends, so it won't be too bad!"

Almost tearfully I thanked him and said I would think about it. After they left, I thought about when he had said and decided to move in with Cecil—why waste time? I immediately wrote to Johnny and told him to tell Cecil I would move in. The following Friday I did, and Cecil was waiting for me when I arrived.

I began to relax completely for the first time since I could remember. Things were so quiet and pleasant in that tiny room, which Cecil had furnished in such excellent taste. He only came Friday nights and would leave on Sunday. What more could I ask for? I bought a TV set, an iron, and ironing board, and began to set up my little housekeeping. I had friends over to watch TV, and that kept me in quite a bit. I introduced Cecil to Eddie, whom I had met shortly after I broke off with Bill Lopez, and they seemed to click. When they were together on weekends, out I would go to a movie, visiting, or just for a walk. Sex was not that important, but I did manage to snatch a piece now and then—mostly then! Nevertheless, little as it was, with my luck I contracted VD, and days were spent going to and from the doctor's office. My doctor was gay and a very pleasant man. He was quite charming and all business, which I appreciated.

During this period the Bal Fantastique was upon us once more. Again, I took my white evening gown and cut it into a bathing suit, wore a cap-cut "party wig" in light green, and a red overskirt. Joe wore his long, red wig and a bathing suit, over which he had a black and flesh-colored cape. At the ball, all I could drink were sodas because of the injections I was receiving.

At one point when Joe and I were walking around, we met a guy dressed as Castro in a fatigue suit and hat. He asked me, "Did you come as Martha Washington?"

"Yes," I said. "Didn't she always wear a bathing suit and show her legs?" *Idiot!* I thought.

Joe and I were asked to pose for pictures and obliged willingly. I had an enjoyable evening but would have enjoyed it more had I been able to drink a little, especially in drag.

Rog wrote me and told me he was coming to New York for training. He arrived May 8, earlier than expected. We made the usual rounds of the bars, and the week seemed to fly. The following Sunday, bright and early he woke, dressed, said good-bye, and was gone. Later that day, I helped George paint the new apartment he had just taken on West Ninetieth Street, just around the corner from Cecil's place. The next few days were spent in papering and finishing his apartment. This apartment building was to become very important to me, but as yet I naturally wasn't aware of it.

I remained at Cecil's from March till mid-June. About this time, we both felt that because of Eddie on the scene, Cecil needed more privacy, and I decided to look for another place. I found a small furnished apartment three houses from where George was living. It wasn't much, but it was a place I could finally call my own. I promptly took it and was once again the gypsy on the move.

George and I flew to Washington in June to help Rog

celebrate his birthday. Since mine was two days later, it was to be a joint celebration, and Rog had a party at the cabin at Chesapeake Bay. There weren't too many people because of the sleeping arrangements, but we managed to have a wonderful time and hated leaving.

Johnny Parks came and went on the weekends that followed and stayed with me. I started to develop a new set of friends, due to the fact I was now a regular of a new bar called the C'est Soir. There was Johnny Edison, a Puerto Rican boy, about eighteen, who was very sweet and innocent-looking and very nice. We became very friendly and whenever we went out, people took us for lovers. Through him I met Joe Nickolie, an Italian and very sexy-looking young man, and several other people. There were so many guys named John, that we finally had to call them by number so we would know about whom we were talking.

My 1959 vacation was spent again in AC. As usual, the meeting of many nice people led to arrangements to meet over Labor Day, and many of the people I had met during my vacation were there. Together we went to dinner, the beach, and in general had a good time. It was so crowded that George and I decided to leave a day earlier to avoid some of the rush. However, we learned that the Halloween ball was to be held October 24, and plans were in the works once we returned home.

George decided this time to go in drag as well, and so the three of us, Joe, George, and I, made plans to attend. I wore a shoulder-length platinum blond, Marilyn Monroe–type wig, tight wine-colored Lurex dress slit to the top of the right leg; George was in a short, brown-streaked wig, pink sequined bathing suit, and long black cape; Joe in his extra-long brown wig with bangs, page-boy style, and flesh-colored bathing suit and floor-length, sheer, see-through nylon black gown, we left for the dance. We looked great but didn't enter the Grand March as usual.

The following Saturday I was invited to a costume party in Brooklyn Heights. I wore Joe's wig and the dress from the week before. I had asked Jody, a boy I had met a few months earlier, to escort me. When he got the cab, the driver wouldn't take five people, and he took one himself. I realized driving in our cab that I should have been with him and wondered how I managed to be in the one in which I was now. I felt terrible and was relieved when he showed up ten minutes after we arrived.

The evening went along very smoothly until George arrived from another party in the neighborhood and said the people at the party at which he was wanted to see me, so we went back to the first party for awhile. While there, Jody met and was talking with several people, and since it was getting late, I asked him to finish his conversation because we had to return to the original party. He resented the fact that I was "dragging him away," and we argued all the way back to the party.

When we returned, we continued to argue. Jody was, of course, feeling no pain from the liquor, and I was right there with him, which I attributed was the main cause of our arguing. Finally, he said he was leaving, and I told him it was all right by me since George would take me home. He grabbed me and said, "You know, you bitch, I've fallen for you!"

That's all I needed to hear! We kissed, and all seemed well for the rest of the evening. He escorted me home and spent the night, and, again I thought things might work out. However, I was wrong, as usual, and with time Jody faded like so many others.

Johnny Parks wrote and asked if he could stay with me until he found a place in New York. It was only to be a temporary arrangement. However, we didn't seem to get along that well, and he found his own apartment shortly after.

Thanksgiving evening after I returned from my parents', I was at home when Johnny Edison called and asked what I was doing. I told him I had no plans, and he suggested going to the drag ball, but I was against it. I had nothing to wear, I told him, and, besides, the wig wasn't even set. He insisted and came over. He had never been in drag and had made a white satin sheath and didn't want to go alone. After several drinks, I told him I would go and called Shelly to escort us.

That evening I must have looked like Bette Davis on a bad night. The red wig was long and ratty looking, and weeks before I had borrowed a black street-length dress from a girl I knew, and off we went. Later, as we were leaving the dance, I was talking with Shelly and Johnny and walked too close to the crowd. A black youth, obviously with long fingernails, snatched off my wig, which wasn't securely fastened to my own hair. I stood there with short hair as the crowd roared. A policeman standing nearby asked what was wrong, and I told him. He said to the man, "Give her back her wig!"

"I didn't take no wig, mister!" he replied.

"Just give it back," the policeman responded.

Then the wig was handed to me. Not bothered by the whole incident and a bit high anyway, I simply shook the wig and placed it on my head, to the delight of the crowd. I smiled, and we hailed a taxi and returned to my apartment and took pictures.

Several days later when I saw the pictures, I said to Johnny, "And you let me go out looking like that? How could you? I'll never live it down!"

"Come on, Tommy, it wasn't *that* bad. Besides, we had a ball, didn't we?" he replied.

"Yep! I suppose we did."

New Year's Eve of 1959–60 was spent at a party given by two lovers by the name of Clyde and Bernie. They had a very large apartment on Third Avenue and suggested we ask whomever we wanted. A few weeks before, Rog had asked me to come to Washington for the holiday, and I told him I would. However, when this party came up, I thought it better to be in New York with all my close friends and called Rog and told him I couldn't make it. He said he was sorry, but that we should try to get together soon. The party was beautiful, and I met some very interesting people.

Clyde and Bernie also threw a party for George on his birthday in February. They supplied the liquor and food, and we had a great time. They, too, liked the idea of giving parties, and who were we to object?

My last trip to the Bal Fantastique was with Joe, both of us in red wigs. I wore the wine-colored dress from AC, and this time my makeup was done very theatrically. Joe wore a black bathing suit with black tights and a long theater coat.

Again, pictures were taken, and at the dance someone asked us to pose for movies. Stars that we were, we camped and carried on for the benefit of the cameras. All in all, it was better than the year before. This time, at least, I could have a few drinks, which does make the difference.

Through one of George's customers, we subleased an apartment on East Fourteenth Street and moved in. It was a beautiful apartment, completely furnished, but there were two lamps and a chair that George referred to as the "McKinley stinkers" because they were awful. They were immediately put in the closet, out of sight.

Bill Bushe gave a party a few days before he was to leave on a European vacation. I wanted to attend in drag, and George forbade me to dress at the apartment because of the fact that too many people would see me on the elevator. However, he did my wig, and I dressed at a friend's house.

When we arrived at Bill's he was shocked, but the rest of the people seemed to enjoy it, and we had a ball camping. One man kept getting me drinks and lighting my cigarettes. At one point in the evening while I was seated on his lap, right after a picture was taken, I said, "You know, you don't have to keep getting me drinks. I don't mind!"

To which he replied, "I always treat a lady with respect!"

"That's very nice," I said, "but, honey, I'm no lady, I'm a man!"

With that he gently pushed me off his lap, and I landed on the floor. The others laughed, and Bill said, "See, that's what you get!"

When the party was over, George and I left together. It was very late now, and it seemed all right that I return to the apartment. There shouldn't be anyone in the elevators at this hour, so we took a taxi home. As we entered the elevator, a middle-aged couple joined us. The lady made the usual small talk, and I just nodded. Fortunately, we only had three floors to go, so I'm sure she didn't think anything of my silence. Besides, I looked good and knew it.

Bill Bushe and I had been attending parties every Friday night given by a black friend of mine named Ernie, with whom I had slept some time before because he was a beautiful-looking man. We would learn the new dances and were anxious to meet new people.

One morning after I returned home from the party, I went into the bedroom that George and I shared, and he had someone with him. I knew who it was! It was a beautiful Italian boy named Bob Lanza, whom I had met a few weeks before when I was with George in the Village. They had been seeing each other, but I knew it wasn't a serious romance—sex, pure and simple! I went to bed since I was very tired. Next afternoon, as I was waking up, I looked over at the other bed and saw Bob looking back. We smiled at each other and said good morning and continued small talk. One thing led to another, and he wound up in my bed, we had wonderful sex, and I asked him to stay for dinner.

When George arrived home he was surprised that Bob was still there.

"I asked him to stay for dinner!" I said.

"Okay," he said, and when Bob was in the bathroom,

added, "I don't mind you balling my trick and asking him to dinner, but I have to cook, too!"

I knew what he meant and also knew he wasn't angry, and we both smiled. In fact, he was glad because he told me that Bob was a wonderful person. I was beginning to see that for myself! We began seeing each other starting the very next day. I liked him, and I knew the feeling, for once, was returned. He worked as a hat-check boy for the Copa and would come over after work every night.

In June I attended a party given by a friend in Long Island and with the pool and beautiful people had a wonderful afternoon. Later in the month Bill took me to see *Gypsy,* with Ethel Merman, for my birthday.

July Fourth was back in AC with George. One afternoon we returned from the beach early, and instead of going home to change as we usually did, we went directly to the bar. It had just opened, and no customers had arrived yet, only the owner. I went to the men's room to wash some of the suntan lotion off my face, when I heard the owner yell, "Jennie, tell Miss Harlow not to dirty the john. I just cleaned it!"

Where have I heard that name before in reference to me? I smiled to myself.

George started to repeat what the owner had said, and I told him I had heard. We both laughed, finished in the men's room, and went to the bar for some drinks. By this time several customers had arrived. When the weekend was over and a few tricks down the drain, we returned to New York with plans of going to Fire Island in August.

During this time Bobby and I were still seeing one another, mostly on weekends, when I wasn't away. I had no desire to be with anyone else and was very happy with him.

SIXTEEN

The apartment was getting to be too expensive for me, so in August I moved to Brooklyn, where my parents were now living.

We went to Fire Island, as planned, the last week of August. I hadn't been there in seven years! The Island had changed, but it was an enjoyable weekend nonetheless. The following weekend we were to house guest with Bill Lopez, Bob, and Phil.

To get to the Island you had to take the train to Sayville, and then a boat to the Island. On the train going out, George and I wanted a drink. We hadn't cups or mixers and then spotted the water cooler. We used the cups and mixed our vodka with water. When we arrived, we weren't feeling any pain. Bob met us at the dock and took us to the house. When we got there, Bill was seated at the long bar in a black, strapless corset, high heels, and makeup. "Good evening, girls. About time you got here!"

We had something to eat, and after Bill had changed, we hit the bars.

The following afternoon I returned alone from the beach early. I wanted to take a shower, but there wasn't one. I thought for a few minutes, then I spotted a large basin and decided I'd make the most of it. I filled it with water and took it to the tiny bathroom and started my "bath." I was halfway through and doing a good job, I thought, not even spilling a drop of water on the floor when Bill came in and saw me.

"What are you doing?" he asked, looking at me seated in the small basin.

"Taking a bath! What does it look like?"

"You know, I never thought of that! Leave it to you, Miss Devlin! You have all the answers!" he said, smiling. "When you're through, I think I'll do the same."

When I finished, Bill followed the same procedure. I started to dress and looked in the bathroom to see how he was doing and started to laugh just as George, Bob, and Phil came in from the beach.

"What's so funny, Tom?" Bob asked.

"Come here, you won't believe this!" I said, still laughing at what I had seen.

When they looked and saw Bill, he had one leg in the toilet bowl, the other out over the basin, and water all over the place. Everyone started laughing as he turned to us and said, "I don't know how she does it! She didn't spill one drop of water, and look—I'm practically drowning! How do you do it, Tommy?"

Of course, we all realized he had done this on purpose to get a laugh, and he succeeded, but we kept it up.

"He's just more clever than you, Bill," said George.

"Anyone would be more clever than Bill," echoed Bob.

"Oh, don't be so hard on him, fellas," Phil said smiling, "he can't help it if he can't do anything right!"

Bill just gave us a funny look and said, "Okay, okay, leave me alone so I can finish. Get out! You hear? Get out!"

We left the bathroom still laughing and went to the counter bar and mixed some drinks.

The following afternoon we were invited to a party. Bill decided he would go in drag. He had on a short blonde wig, red flapper dress, high heels—the works! After we arrived at the party and everyone had gotten over his outfit, he sat on top of the upright piano, singing at the top of his lungs. It was a fun-filled afternoon, and later, Bill was behind me as we all backed out of the house saying our farewells. Not seeing him, I bumped into him, and he lost his balance. I turned and tried to catch him, but it was too late, he had fallen into the sand. All I wound up with was his wig in my hand. We looked down, and there he was, lying in the sand, wigless, with his legs up in the air, a white, ghostlike made-up face staring at us.

"You pushed me!" he said. "You did it deliberately! You can't stand anyone being more gorgeous than you!"

All we could do was stand on the path and laugh. Bob jumped down and helped him up, and after he had put his wig back on, we continued laughing back to the house, while Bill kept repeating, "You pushed me, I know you did! Just 'cause I'm so gorgeous!"

I told him, "Please Bill, my sides! I can't take much more of this. Stop already!"

The incident was to become one of our most pleasant memories!

Bill left that evening, and George, Bob, Phil, and I stayed over for another night. The following day we took pictures in the many beautiful sweaters that Bill had at the house. We took turns posing in them.

"Wait till he sees these," said Bob, "he'll flip!"

As we were about to board the boat back to the mainland, I ran into someone I hadn't seen for some time. We were both friends of Pat, and I asked how he was.

"Haven't you heard, Tommy," he said. "Pat died last month of a heart attack!"

I couldn't believe what I had just heard. Pat was only twenty-six, and of a heart attack—it didn't seem possible! He continued to tell me that Pat had had the attack and was starting to recover when he took a turn for the worse. He also told me that he had married and was the father of a little girl. I was sick all the way home thinking about it. When I returned I sent a Mass card to his family. It wasn't much, but I wanted to show my respect.

George called the owner of the West Ninetieth Street

building to see if she had any vacancies because the rent was becoming too much for him to handle alone. In October, a large apartment one flight up became available. It was furnished, and the two twin beds were brand new, having been purchased after the former tenant moved. He called me and told me about it. I thought it was a good idea, and the rent seemed reasonable, so we took the apartment.

For the October ball, Bill Bushe, who had never been in drag, decided to join me. Phil and Bob were to be our escorts. It was held at the Manhattan Center on West Thirty-fourth Street. Again, we posed for pictures, and later in the evening we were invited to a party in the Village. I wore the black street dress I had borrowed from a girlfriend, which I had worn once before.

As we entered the top floor loft, we were supposed to sign up as the name of the person we were imitating. I couldn't imagine who I looked like until Bill suggested the actress Paulette Goddard. I didn't think I looked like her, but with the wig done the way she usually wore it in her films, I probably could get away with it, so I signed that name.

I ran into Bobby Lanza and was surprised and pleased. At one point in the evening, Bill went to a corner and started rolling down his stockings. I asked him what was wrong.

"Honey, I've had runs in them for days. Be better without them." He smiled while taking them off and stuffing them into his purse.

A few hours later we all left, and Bob drove us home. Bobby fell asleep on my shoulder in the car and was in that position as the final picture of the evening was taken. When he saw it a few days later, he asked why I hadn't wakened him so we could have taken it together. "You looked so cute, I didn't want to," I replied.

Shortly before Christmas I learned one evening in a bar of the death of another friend. Again I was both shocked and upset. Two in one year! It seemed unreal.

The last two weeks of December I was on vacation. I had

been having trouble with my immediate supervisor. We were very friendly outside the office and would go drinking often after work. But at work, whenever she had trouble with her boyfriend, she would take it out on the entire department, including me. I handed in my resignation, effective with the end of my vacation.

The approaching of New Year's Eve 1960–61 was once again the everpresent mixup of what to do for the evening. A party or parties were sure to come along but so far nothing. They began dribbling in. Thinking to avoid bad feelings and wanting to be with all our friends, George and I gave, what, by now, was our annual bottle party. We invited about twenty people. Of course, everyone seemed to bring a friend or two, so about fifty people showed up. Around 1:30, we broke the party up and took cabs downtown to another party. When we arrived, the place was so crowded we could hardly get in the door, so we just stayed for one drink. It was raining very heavily, and we again took a cab to a friend of Bill Lopez's by the name of Don. We sat around drinking and letting the mellowness of the evening drift by. Again, at the witching hour of 6:00 A.M., tired, cold, and quite high, I arrived home, went to bed, and fell asleep immediately.

January second Helenmae gave a party at her home in New Jersey. It had been decided by everyone that the theme would be a hat party. I looked terrible in hats, so when I arrived, I went into another room, took off my shoes, and put on a pair of high heels that had two large red feathers on them. When I came out and went downstairs to the basement where the party was being held, everyone laughed and made their comments. "Leave it to Miss D! Gotta be different!"

After we had been there a while, I changed shoes, as the others took off their hats.

I looked in the papers for a job but couldn't find anything that appealed to me, so I registered with a part-time agency. I went from office to office for about three weeks. During the third week, a real estate firm for which I was working asked if I would like the position on a permanent basis. The work wasn't hard. I was now doing dictaphone typing and was more or less on my own; the salary was decent, so I accepted the position.

I learned that my friend Alan hadn't died. He had been very ill, but fortunately was well now. Although I didn't know where he was, I felt much better just knowing he was all right.

I tried to give up smoking and became hard to live with; I was very bitchy most of the time. Nothing terribly exciting was happening. Bobby and I had broken up after his vacation to the West Coast. He had met someone out there and decided to move permanently. I was upset, but it seemed each time something like this happened, the hurt wasn't quite as bad as before. I made frequent trips to the bars, a few trips to the baths, but still felt as though I were in a rut. Same old thing day in and out. How tiresome!

In June, George decided he wanted to live alone and took an apartment on East Eighty-seventh Street. I could easily afford the rent on my apartment, so I stayed. I met a boy named Wayne, and he moved in, strictly on a roommate basis. He had a lover with whom I didn't get along, and so after a month I asked him to move.

One evening I ran into Sal in a restaurant, and we talked for some time. He was living alone and wanted to move. Wayne was still living with me, so I asked the owner if she had any vacancies. She did, a very tiny room upstairs, and Sal took it. Sal and I flew to Washington a few weeks later for the weekend once again to celebrate my birthday and Rog's. Shortly after our return, Wayne moved, and Sal and I became roommates.

Sal came home one evening and said he had looked at a very nice apartment on West Eighty-sixth Street and wanted to take it. When I first saw it, I liked it and told Johnny Parks I would be moving. He had expressed his interest in my apartment many times and had told me if I ever decided to move, he would gladly take it. Sal and I moved to the Eighty-sixth Street apartment.

We were there about a month, and the rent was due, but Sal didn't have it. "I'll have to make a phone call," he said one evening.

I knew what that meant and had been hoping perhaps we might get back together. I saw now it was a lost cause. He hadn't changed a bit. I also realized that I would be in this situation every month, unless he got himself a permanent job. I was sick with worry because of what I had done: I had left a beautiful apartment and really wasn't that happy in the new one. I had done it only because of Sal. Now, I didn't know what to do. I called the owner of the Ninetieth Street building to ask if she had any vacancies. Unfortunately, she didn't. I spoke with Johnny Parks about it, and he told me that the girl in the front apartment on his floor was going on vacation to Europe for a few months and wanted to sublease her place. I spoke with her, and it was decided I would take over for her. She said she was leaving in a few days and could stay with friends if I wanted to take the apartment that weekend. I agreed and informed my present landlord that I was moving, and that Sal would take over the remainder of the lease. I moved at the end of the month into the small front-room apartment on West Ninetieth Street.

The garden apartment on the ground floor became available, and Johnny took it with a friend. I moved back into the old apartment number 2 in which I had formerly lived with George. You can see now why I said this building would become important to me. Again, things seemed to be going well for me.

My parents and I were in the process of buying a home in Babylon, Long Island, and the final papers were almost ready. However, in September my sister Pat, shortly after her fifteenth birthday, was hit by an automobile and hospitalized. After her release, my parents moved to the Long Island home.

At the end of October, with Johnny as my escort, I attended

the ball at Manhattan Center. Joe made my gown. It was a lavender strapless sheath with light grey chiffon panels in the rear. George, as usual, did the long red wig, and in a gold evening coat to the floor that I had borrowed from Marie, I left with them for the dance. We ordered drinks, and as I was walking up some steps on the upper floor, I slipped slightly, causing the drink to splatter in my face. We went to a corner, and Johnny took a tissue and very lightly tried to dry my face without removing any makeup. I then went to the powder room, rechecked the makeup, and it seemed fine. Was I that high? I had better watch it, especially in high heels!

The following evening we were invited to a party in the Village, and Johnny again escorted me. I wore the same outfit as the evening before, and George did the wig slightly differently. I met many old friends who complimented me on how well I looked.

I took some pinup pictures at the apartment as a camp, and when two of them turned out well, had them made as Christmas cards, which I sent to very close friends. One friend called after he received it and said, "I opened your card as I was going down the subway steps on the way to work, and when I saw it, I laughed so hard I almost fell down the stairs. You're too much!"

I was pleased he took it the way it was intended—as a camp!

Joe and I registered for hairdressing school the beginning of December and were to start right after the New Year. So many of our friends were hairdressers, and both of us wanted to know more about the field with the possibility of entering it after completion of the course.

New Year's Eve 1961–62 we were invited to a party at a friend of George's on West Eighty-third Street. I made Black Russians at home and took them with me to the party. I was seated on the couch and had about seven drinks. Shortly after the New Year came in, I got up to get another drink and almost fell on my face. I was stoned! They had a way of sneaking up on me, and I didn't realize it until I stood up. I felt ill, and later after I threw up in the bathroom, told the host I was going home. As I was leaving the elevator, I met Johnny Edison, who had moved to Rochester with the company he was now working for, and was in town for the holidays. He asked me where I was going and what was wrong.

"I don't feel well," I said. "I'm going home!"

"It's early yet! Wait, I'll go with you! Maybe the walk will do you good."

"No, you go to the party and have a good time. It's really nice. Lots of new faces, but I'm just not with it tonight."

He insisted he go with me, and after we walked home in the light snow, I showered, changed, and had something to eat, after which I felt like a new person and was ready to go again. It was such a beautiful night when we left my apartment to return to the party, that we walked through Central Park. The snow had stopped, and the moonlight on the white snow looked like a picture postcard. It wasn't cold, and we walked arm in arm through the park until we arrived at Eighty-third Street. We went back to the party, and I drank sodas the rest of the evening. A friend of mine who lived in Toronto had arrived while I was home changing, and he spent the night with me after the party.

Joe and I started hairdressing school the first week in January, and in my first class, to my delight, was Ray, a young man I had known for some time. I hadn't seen him since the time I had brought Bobby Garcia to his party years before. He had started a few weeks ahead of us and was about to enter his next class. However, we were in the same class about a week before he moved on, and we saw each other daily.

Because I was so busy with school and work, the months slipped by. I met a boy named John Winthrop in a movie one evening, and we began seeing one another. One night after

George and I had been to the theater where we saw *No Strings,* we decided to go to the baths. There I met someone and went home with him. When I ran out of cigarettes, he gave me a pack he had and a book of matches with his initials on it. The following Saturday, John and I were going out, and he came to my apartment. As I reached for a book of matches to light my cigarette, I noticed they were the same matches I had gotten from the guy from the baths. The end result was that John had been with him the evening before and left his cigarettes there. We didn't have to argue! We both knew that we had cheated on one another and decided it would be better not to see each other on a steady basis. So, again, I had another friend!

The lease was up on the apartment George was living in on the East Side, so once again he moved in with me. The week before we were to fly to Washington to celebrate both my birthday and Roger's, my sister was invited to her boyfriend's prom, and dressed at our apartment. George did her hair, and we took movies and still pictures. After she left for the prom, we finished the reel in my apartment.

A few weeks later, George, Bill, and I were invited to a Christmas in July party on the Lower East Side. It was on the ground floor, and the young hoods in the neighborhood started bothering the guests who were arriving, so the host called the police. Instead of telling the kids to cool it, they arrested the people at the party for "disorderly conduct." I saw this as I was in the hall and went to the roof with a few other guests and looked over the rooftop in time to see Bill and George getting into a police van. Thinking it was now safe, we went to another building, down the stairs, and into the street.

We were walking up the street, when one of the cops stopped us and lined us up with the others. Next thing, we, too, were in the wagon and off to jail. Next day we were fined ten dollars for disorderly conduct and released. Bill was a nervous wreck, but George and I survived. After all, it was my third trip, and I was sort of used to it at this point! I knew they couldn't do much more than fine us, so I wasn't that concerned. What pissed everyone off was the fact that *we* had called the police, and they'd arrested us instead of the hoods. Some justice system!

On August 4th, movie star Marilyn Monroe died. Joe and I, at this time, were in the touch-up class and refused to work on any light blond customers. It was just an excuse, but we stuck to it for a week!

In late October, Joe made me a strapless, pink brocade tight evening gown with a large taffeta, red overskirt. George did my blonde wig in the latest style, and I borrowed a mink stole from a friend. Little Ray and another friend, Frank, had planned on going with me in drag as well. After we were at the dance for about an hour, I noticed the police taking some guests who were in very scanty costumes from the premises. I didn't pay too much attention to it and was talking with a group of straight men and women seated at a table near the orchestra. Ray and Frank were busy dancing, and then I heard the dance was being raided.

Not again, I thought. "Damn! Now what do I do?" I said to a woman seated near me.

"Look, honey, you're dressed very well and could easily pass for one of us. Why not leave with my husband and the rest of our group?" she suggested.

"Thank you. But I can hardly do that! I'm in evening wear, and you people aren't. They'll suspect something!"

"Pull up your dress a bit before you get to the cop at the door!" she said.

"With these hairy legs," I smiled, "not a chance!"

I heard the police were charging fifty dollars to anyone who wanted to leave by the side exit. None of us had that kind of money so I prepared myself for what I thought was about to happen. We waited for about an hour, and no one approached us. Then slowly we made our way to the entrance and saw a police van outside. We watched a few drags leave, and the policeman just turned his head as they left. We waited a bit longer. I didn't trust what I had seen. Finally, I turned to Ray and Frank and said, "Let's chance it! What can we lose?"

Slowly we left the dance and passed the policeman, who just glanced our way for a moment and then looked in the opposite direction. We started walking slowly toward Eighth Avenue. When we had gone about half a block, I looked back and saw that things seemed normal. Then we hailed a cab and went to my apartment to change.

"I heard on the radio about the raid," George said to me the following day. "I thought you were in it. Glad to see you weren't!"

We later learned that they had only taken people with obscene outfits. Another close call!

A week later, John Winthrop gave a party that Frank and I attended in drag. I had cut the evening gown to street length, and since the wig was still freshly done, wore it again. We had a great time, and at the end of the evening, I had an argument with a friend because he was trying to make someone I was interested in. That blew over very quickly after we returned to my apartment. *Typical evening,* I thought later. *Bitches everywhere! Oh, well!*

I finally got in touch with Alan, whom I thought had died, and invited him for Thanksgiving dinner at my parents' home in Long Island.

There was just one month left of schooling, and I would be finished, but I was tired between work and school all year, so I took the month of December off to rest. I planned on returning in January to finish.

New Year's Eve of 1962–63 we gave our party, which turned out better than some years before. Later that evening, at a bar, I once again ran into my friend Bill from Toronto, and we spent the night together. Too bad it had to be a year apart; he was good in bed!

I returned to school in January and graduated on the 28th. In April, I was out of work for 7-1/2 days due to a severe cold, which I contracted at work. So on the 15th, I was fired and started immediately to collect unemployment. During this time, I went to the beach whenever I could with George on his days off, and, in general, took things easy.

A few weeks later, I was called into the office at the unemployment board and asked if I was working as a hairdresser. I told them I wasn't and didn't have a license, which was true. They had to check with Albany to be sure, I was told. They did, and for two weeks I was unable to collect until word came that there was no license issued to me. No money was coming in, and the landlady was very nice after I explained what had happened. She told me not to worry. Since I was accused of working as a hairdresser, through a friend I took a job in the Bronx as one, although I hated it from the very first day. I was receiving a small salary and once again collecting unemployment. Meantime, I was looking in the papers for a permanent position.

Once again, in June George and I flew to Washington. While Rog was at work on afternoon, we decided it was about time we did a bit of sightseeing. Most of the places of interest had very long lines, and we didn't want to wait. We took movies and still pictures and visited museums and the home of George Washington in Mount Vernon.

I finally secured a job with a law firm in August, working nights. The job was easy, and everyone seemed to get along well with one another. I had to adjust my lifestyle because now everything I had done in the past had to be reversed.

For Halloween, I gave a "Stars of the '40s" party. I wanted everyone to come in costume as a movie star of the 1940s. Nostalgia wasn't to become popular for several years, but I always liked that era and thought for a change it might be interesting to have a theme. Naturally, I went as Betty Grable, who had been my idol for many years. I was extremely pleased when almost all the guests showed up in keeping with the theme.

Early in the evening, I ran out of ice and asked Johnny Tyler if he would get some for me. He wanted me to go with him, so I took off my black skirt and put on a street-length skirt. I naturally had to remove the feathers from my hair as well. We drove several blocks to a bar I knew. I waited in the car while he went in and got the ice. After we returned to the apartment, several guests had arrived. Most of the people I didn't recognize at first. We had Vivian Blaine, Vera Ralston, Lucille Ball, Sara Allgood, Illona Massey, Bea Lillie, two boys dressed as sailors from *Anchor's Aweigh,* a cowboy, the one and only Marlene, and a host of others. We took pictures and had a great time. I was very pleased with the evening. One of the guests who came as Lucille Ball, to whom I loaned two small attachments, I didn't recognize at all. He was a singer friend of mine, whom I shall call Cliff Wayne. I had never seen him in drag before, and he looked marvelous. This young man a few years later was to become a star in his own right—as I always felt he would.

On November 22 President Kennedy was shot, and I was so upset I took off from work. For three days we watched television, as millions all over the world did. That something so shocking, so unbelievable could have happened in our lifetime was uppermost in the minds of everyone. Even during the Christmas holidays, no one seemed to have the usual holiday spirit, and it became just another day to many people.

My brother was in the army and came home for Christmas. As in the past, I always managed to be home for both Thanksgiving and Christmas dinners. My father had told me years before, "I don't care what you do or where you go, but I'd like you home for either Thanksgiving or Christmas, preferably both. If you can't make both, please try for at least one of them. It's not asking much, but I do like all of us together for one of them."

I made that promise to him and have never broken it, even after he died. Only after Mom died did I stop going "home."

New Year's Eve of 1963–64 was, as before, held at our apartment.

SEVENTEEN

In January, I took a full-time day position with a hotel as a reservationist for the upcoming World's Fair. I resigned the evening full-time position and worked for them on a part-time basis, four nights a week. It was a bit hectic working so much, but the extra money helped.

In the early spring, George moved to Detroit with a man he met and was to live there for some time. I had the apartment once again to myself. My next-door neighbor Jim told me the day that George left that he, too, was moving. He was tired of New York and was moving to San Francisco. A short time later, he, too, left, and Johnny Parks and I were the only gay people left in the building.

In June my sister Pat graduated from high school. She selected the type of dress she wanted to wear, and Joe made it for her. Prom night Bobby Garcia and I went to Long Island so he could do her hair. I had rented a white stole for her, and she looked just beautiful!

When most of the reservations had been completed toward the end of the first year of the World's Fair, the manager told me I would have to return to the lobby. I was in a room upstairs all by myself and loved it. I could come and go as I pleased, and no one said a word. Returning to the lobby would mean I would have to join the union, which I was against doing, so I resigned in September and returned full-time to the night position.

In October, I secured a job as a superintendent in a nine-family furnished apartment building on West 107th Street and moved from the Ninetieth Street apartment. It was a very easy job with little to do, and I still had my evening position. I lived rent free and had a small monthly salary, and everything, for a change, seemed to be great.

In December, my brother and his wife had a baby girl. They had been married earlier in the year somewhere in Tennessee. I was delighted at being an uncle (or aunt, whatever the case) for the first time and was looking forward to meeting my new sister-in-law and my new niece.

New Year's Eve of 1966–65 was the quietest I had ever spent. My friend Frank de Sal, whom I hadn't seen in many years because he had moved to Florida, was home visiting his parents for the holidays and called me. Along with a friend of his, he came to my apartment, and the three of us welcomed the New Year. Later, we went to a party in the West Seventies. Although it was one of the most quiet New Years, it was also one of the most pleasant.

I had been going for quite some time, usually on Sundays, to the movies, cruising. Occasionally, I would go to the baths. In early January at the baths one evening, I met Guy Pierre and took him to my apartment. Later, we talked for some time, and somehow it was arranged he would stay with me for awhile. He was very interested in tape recordings, which I knew nothing about, and explained the workings of them. Eventually I, too, purchased a recorder with his help, recording all my old records onto the tapes. It would save space, and once recorded, they were permanent.

I ran into Sal, again and he invited me to a costume party at his house. I wore my Grable outfit, and Guy escorted me. It was a pleasant evening with nothing out of the ordinary. Guy stayed with me for about a month then moved. Oh, but what a month! No love, but the sex was great! I heard from George, and he was coming back to New York because his mother was ill. He was due to arrive in early spring. Meantime, I met another man named Terry who was from Ohio originally and had just moved to New York, and he stayed with me about month. We had a brief sexual thing but were not lovers or anything like that.

One afternoon, my sister Pat called me and said she wanted to see me. I knew right away she had something she wanted to discuss and told her to come up. She took an extended lunch hour and after lunch, I said, "Okay, honey! What's up?"

"Well, Phil and I are getting married, and I know you, you'll want a big wedding and the works, but we don't. Just a simple reception with our families."

"That's beautiful! But you have to have some kind of wedding. I mean, Mom would want it, and you can't deny her that."

After we talked a while longer it was decided—with my help—that she would have a small wedding. So, like a "mother of the bride," I started the wheels in motion. After getting all the information, I had the invitations printed and mailed; she made church arrangements, and I asked Bobby Garcia to do her hair. He worked one block from my apartment, so it was agreed she would dress at my place. Then I rented a limousine.

The morning of the wedding, we attended church, after which she went to have her hair done. My mother and sister Mary arrived shortly before she returned from Bobby's.

After she had dressed and pictures were taken, the limousine arrived, and we proceeded to the Bronx. My parents were now living there, having given up the home in Long Island due to the fact my father's place of business was on strike, and little funds were coming in. I escorted her down the aisle because my dad had an artificial leg, having lost it in an accident when I was very young and he didn't want to walk her down because of it. As we were walking down the aisle, I felt a lump in my throat and a tear in my eye but held it back. After the wedding they went to the photographers. At the reception later, my mother, who was not a drinker by any means, got a bit high because someone had put liquor in her beer when she wasn't looking. Needless to say, I was completely out of it! So much that at one point in the evening when I was dancing, I slipped and almost took the poor woman I was dancing with to the floor with me. But all in all, we had a marvelous time.

While working part-time for an agency, I secured a position with a travel agency on West Forty-second Street. It was part-time, and I enjoyed the work. Although I knew absolutely nothing about the field, I learned quickly. It had many advantages, such as discounts on hotels and air travel, so I decided to try and hold on to it as long as possible.

Labor Day, Bill Bushe and I went to a gay resort upstate. It was a beautiful place, but there were hardly any guests, so we did our best to make the most of the weekend.

Toward the end of November my sister Pat had a baby girl. With my brother, I now had two nieces. I had been godfather to my brother's child before Pat's wedding, and now she asked me again to be godfather, which I gladly accepted.

I spent Christmas at home and New Year's Eve of 1965–66 was spent at a friend's on East Twenty-third Street. George was in Detroit on vacation.

In January, Mary, my youngest sister, informed me she was getting married and her boyfriend asked me to be best man. I rented a car through a friend, and since I didn't have a driver's license, asked him to drive me. We were so late in picking up Pat and Phil that by the time we arrived at Mary's, she was already married. Oh, well! Pat and I were still the matron of honor and best man, although now it was by proxy.

In early May I went to a party in the Village. It was quite crowded, and the apartment beneath was vacant. I saw several people going onto the fire escape and down the stairs to the apartment below, and, being naturally nosey, followed! They went into the apartment, which was in total darkness, and were having sex. I had met a guy earlier by the name of Stan Gordon, whom, I liked very much. He was in the vacant apartment as well, and we started to carry on. After a few minutes, it became so warm that I left and went upstairs. When the party broke up, I stayed with one of the hosts and slept with him. In the morning, when I woke, I was in bed with the other host and on seeing him, just smiled. After breakfast I went home.

For Memorial Day, Stan Gordon invited me to his house in Long Island. It was small and faced the canal. He invited several people over and we had an afternoon party in the backyard. I hadn't laughed so much in years! He was one of the most comical people I had ever met and he kept all of us laughing practically the whole time I was there.

In June, Bill Bushe, George and I went to Fire Island. My birthday was coming soon, and as much as I hated to admit it, it was to be my thirty-sixth birthday—where did the years go? The host of the house at which we were staying told me they were having a cocktail party that afternoon and asked if I would go over to another house and pick up something that the gay girls wanted to bring. I did, and during the conversation it came out that this was to be a surprise party for me. I was, of course, delighted—since this time I hadn't planned it as I had years before.

Later that afternoon, I was coming into the house for something with a drink in my hand, when the host shoved a popper up my nose. I stopped, pulled back, and my head started to spin. Bill didn't like using poppers and was by turned off by the whole incident. After most of the guests had left, George started to prepare dinner, while I went to my room to rest. When dinner was over, Bill said he decided he would return to the city and after saying farewell to everyone, left.

That evening after I had dressed, I went outside to wait for the others. It was dark, but the moon was shining brightly. As I was standing by the gate, a young man passed and said hello.

I returned his hello, then he grabbed me and kissed me. I was stunned! Then as fast as he appeared, he was gone down the small path and out of sight. I told the others when they came out what had happened, and looking up and down and seeing no one, thought I had made up the whole story. I decided it was no use to insist, so I dropped the matter.

The Fourth of July I again went to visit Stan for the weekend. As with the first time, he continued to entertain his guests with his comic doings. We went to a few bars out there, and he introduced me to many people. Again, I had a terrific weekend and was sorry it was over so quickly.

Mary's husband phoned me one afternoon to tell me she had had a stillborn baby. When I attended the funeral, my heart almost sank as I saw the tiny white coffin being lowered into the ground. Fortunately, she took the situation very well; much better in fact than I.

Because I was having trouble with the upstairs tenant, I once again decided it was time to move. I looked in the papers and at several apartments. When I saw one on West Eighty-fifth Street, I immediately fell in love with it. It was, in a way, similar to the one I had for some time on West Ninetieth. When I looked at it, there was also a girl interested in it as well. We both had seen one earlier, and she had told the landlord she would take it. Now, on seeing this one, she wanted it. I took the landlord to the side and said, "Look, I like this place. I'll give you a month's rent, right now, in cash, and a check on the signing of the lease!"

He told me he'd have to call his father-in-law, as he was the owner, and discuss the situation with him. When he finished the call, he said, "My father-in-law said, 'Take the man.' So, I guess you have it! What is your name?"

I told him and gave him the money, and he in turn gave me a receipt.

The end of October, my brother's wife had another girl. Now he had two girls, and his family was beginning to increase.

George and I moved to the new apartment November 15.

New Year's Eve of 1966–67 was spent at the apartment of a friend on Third Avenue Gramercy Park Terrace.

In February, George gave a birthday party, and I was to act as a maid. I had the outfit, and two friends of his came to apply my makeup. They were professional makeup men, yet it took almost three hours to apply it. I was supposed to be a black maid, with a French outfit similar to those seen in movies. When it was finished and Bill Lopez arrived, not recognizing me as I let him in and took his coat, he said as he looked around the apartment, "Where's Tommy?"

Still standing with his coat in my arms, I said, "Right here, honey!"

"My God! You look great!"

I looked more like an Italian with a deep sunburn than a black maid, as I was supposed to be. We took pictures, which unfortunately did not come out, for some reason. However, we had an enjoyable afternoon and, later, after I had changed, we all went out to various bars.

One evening when I returned home from work, George had a guest. He introduced me, and I sat down and talked with them for some time. His name was Don Venta. He had a marvelous personality, and we got along beautifully. I was immediately attracted to this young man, not only sexually, but I felt at ease with him. In the weeks that followed, we would run into one another in the street since he lived in the neighborhood, or in the bars, and would stand and talk for hours at a time. We became very close and dear friends and the sexual interest faded.

In July Stan again asked me out, and by now he said I didn't need an invite—that I was just to call and come whenever I wanted to. I enjoyed it there! It was relaxing, and with Stan around, you could be sure of a wonderful time.

The beginning of September Bobby Garcia talked me into

going to Puerto Rico. I had never been there and always wanted to see it, so I agreed. Working for the travel agency was now paying off. Through my boss, I secured complimentary accommodations in one of the largest hotels in the Condado area. There was only one problem. Because of Labor Day, the hotel was completely booked, and we couldn't be taken until after the holiday. I stayed at a guest house while Bobby stayed with friends. When the holiday was over, we moved into the hotel. The room was beautiful but faced the street.

We were there only one day when the assistant manager called one morning. "I'm sorry, Mr. Devlin," she said, "but you're in the wrong room. You should be in ocean view!"

I started to tell her it was all right, that we had unpacked, but she insisted and said she would send someone for our luggage. We threw our things together and were taken two floors higher in the hotel to the same room we had below. I thought it was ridiculous and called the bell captain. It turned out that the bellboy had taken the wrong keys, and we should have been across the hall. The room was really beautiful and faced the ocean and had a balcony. I spent much time during the evening hours on the balcony, just looking at the ocean and the peacefulness of the entire scene.

Shortly after my return from San Juan, my father became very ill and had to have half his stomach removed. It was a serious operation, but, fortunately, he came through it very well. I had suspected he might have cancer, but the doctors informed me this was not the case, so I dismissed that thought.

On October 15, George and I went to the Rivoli theater to see a reissue of the classic film *Gone With the Wind*. We had both seen it many times before, but it was such a beautiful film, we wanted to see it again. After the movie, we went to a bar for a few drinks. I ran into some friends and started chatting with them. A little later, George said he was tired and was going home. I decided to stay a while longer and got home about 3:15 in the morning.

About 6:30 A.M. I woke with terrible stomach pains. I tried to think of what I had eaten that could cause what I believed was a bad gas attack. As soon as the drugstore opened, I had my prescription for gas pills refilled, returned home, and went back to bed. By 11:00 A.M. the pain was worse, and I asked George to take me to a doctor. After examining me the doctor said my blood count was high, and I might have appendicitis. He gave me pills to take and said if the condition worsened, I was to call him, and he would place me in the hospital.

We returned to the apartment, called my office, and told them I was ill and wouldn't be to work that night. By 6:00 P.M., my stomach had blown up so much I could hardly move. I called the doctor and told him I wanted to be placed in the hospital, where proper tests could be taken.

By 7:00 P.M. I was seated in the admitting office of Flower and Fifth Avenue Hospital. My stomach was so blown up that I couldn't close the zipper of my trousers and had to wear a long coat. Afterwards I was taken to my room, which was semiprivate, and told to change. As George was leaving I asked him not to call my parents until the following day, when I would probably know what was wrong. I didn't want them to worry unnecessarily!

After x-rays were taken, I heard one of the doctors say, "Prepare patient for OR at 11:00 P.M."

Then I knew what I had feared: appendicitis! At this point I didn't care what they did as long as I got rid of the pain. Back in my room, an orderly came and shaved me. He started from my knees and worked halfway up my chest. I felt like a plucked chicken! After an injection, I fell asleep. Next, I recall I was being lifted on to a movable bed, and a sheet was put over me. My stomach was sticking so far up in the air that as I was being wheeled to the elevator, I'm sure people in the hall must have thought me on my way to the delivery room. I wasn't fully awake at this point, but when I arrived at the operating room, I saw a nurse with a face mask, and she asked how I was.

"This is my first cut," I recall saying. "Ask them to make it a neat one, please!"

I guess she smiled, I really couldn't tell and nodded. As I was put on the operating table, I saw the clock. 11:00 P.M. exactly! Then several faces appeared, and something black covered my face.

When I awoke, the first thing I saw again was another clock. Midnight! My doctor came to the bed and said, "How are you doing? You know, yours was the largest appendix we've seen in some time: six inches when we unravelled it!"

I recall smiling and then falling asleep. When I awoke again I was back in my room, and it must have been very early in the morning, for it was dark outside. I had to urinate badly and tried to get out of bed to go to the bathroom. We had two, and I started across the room for the nearest one. I almost fainted as my feet hit the floor. As I was halfway across the room, a nurse happened by, and, seeing me, came in. "What are you doing?" she asked.

"I have to urinate!" I told her.

"Why didn't you buzz? That's what we're here for!"

She held my arms while I urinated and then helped me back to bed.

"If you need anything, there's the buzzer. Use it!" She smiled and left the room.

The next day I called George and told him to call my parents. They came the following day, and I was upset with my dad for making the long trip because he had been so sick himself. I convinced them I was fine and not to worry, and when the visiting hours were over, they left. The following day both my sisters came. I had people coming almost daily and the time went by swiftly. After the stitches were taken out on the seventh day, my doctor insisted I stay three more days. I had no choice! I felt fine but had to stay.

When I had finally left the hospital and was still recuperating, Bill Bushe and I flew to San Juan. I had to take it easy, but the rest would do me a world of good, I thought! I never met so many people in my life—and me looking like a plucked chicken with my hairy chest growing in! They should have had a revolving door in our room because people came and went the entire time we were there. It was during this period that I met Jorge, who was to become a good friend.

New Year's Eve of 1967–68 was spent with Bobby Garcia, his friend Tony, and Tony's lover, David. Tony was working in Puerto Rico and had returned with Bobby and me in September. I met David at the airport after we arrived. I stayed at the party for some time, but since I had another party at which I had to make an appearance, I left for a while and returned later to end the evening with my friends.

In February I flew alone to San Juan to visit Jorge, whom, I had met in September. We liked one another very much, and I was tempted to move down but gave the matter second thoughts. He was busy most of the time, and I was alone, so I didn't enjoy myself very much. Every bar I went into I saw nothing but a sea of blonds—and this I didn't need! When the week was over, I bid Jorge farewell and flew back to New York.

The night I returned from San Juan, Bill Lopez called me and asked me to meet him at a bar downtown. He wanted me to meet his new lover, who he said reminded him of me. This I had to see, so I agreed!

When I arrived at the bar with my newly acquired tan in the middle of winter, I did look healthy, and he commented on it. I met Ken and liked him immediately. Physically, we were not alike, but I suppose our personalities were similar. The three of us talked and danced for hours. Ken was out of work, and since we did the same type of work, I told him I would check at my office and see if there were any positions available. I did, and they suggested he come in, which he did, and was hired. Now I had someone with whom I could talk at work when things were slow. Seeing one another daily brought us closer together as friends, and I enjoyed Ken's company very much.

In April my father became very ill again and entered the hospital. This time all of his stomach had to be removed, and he had to be fed through a tube inserted in the stomach. He had lost a tremendous amount of weight, and I feared the worst. I called the social service director of the hospital, and she had my father's doctor call me. He wanted to see me, and we made arrangements for the 25th of April.

I called Pat, and together we went to the hospital. My father had been released and was resting at home. It began to rain very heavily, and, as neither of us had an umbrella, we stopped in a store and bought one. After being introduced to the doctor, he took us to another room so we could talk privately. My heart was beating very fast as so many things were racing through my mind.

After he closed the door, he turned to us. "Mr. Devlin," he began, "your father is a very sick man."

I kept saying to myself, *Please don't let it be cancer. Please, God, anything but that!*

"Your father has terminal cancer!"

There it was! What I had feared for so long was now a reality. Pat and I turned and looked at one another. I saw the tears already forming in her eyes, and I tried hard not to show mine. "Is there any hope?" I managed to get it out.

"None whatever! We had to remove all of his stomach, and he will have to eat through a tube."

"I know that already; I've seen it. How long would you say he has?"

"Six, seven months—eight, tops!"

There was nothing more to say. We thanked him for being

so honest with us and left. I called Mary, who was working, and we met for lunch. When the food arrived, none of us could eat; we just nibbled at it, and Mary returned to work. Pat and I took the subway to my parents' home.

When we arrived, my dad asked, "Well, what did the doctor say?" I couldn't tell him or my mother, for that matter! "He said you had a very serious operation, and it will be awhile before you're strong. Just take it easy and relax," I lied. I wanted to cry but couldn't. Here I was, lying to a dying man. Oh, God forgive me, but I had to!

"Then, why aren't I getting stronger each day?" he finally asked.

"He said it will take time," I answered.

A little later, he went into the living room and lay down on the couch to watch TV and lit a cigarette.

"The doctor said I could smoke as much as I wanted," he said, looking at me, knowing I was about to ask why he was smoking.

He knows! I said to myself. *He knows!*

On the subway going back to Manhattan, I kept thinking of what was going to happen and tried desperately to hold back the tears. When I reached the city, I didn't want to go home and needed to talk to someone. I called Don—my pillar of strength on whom I had come to lean so much—and asked if he was doing anything special. He said he wasn't and asked me over.

I was seated in the living room when he came in with drinks. I took a few sips, but my mind wasn't on the conversation. He asked, "Tommy! What's wrong? Is something bothering you?"

I put down the glass and walked to the window, the tears finally starting to flow. "Oh, Don, my father's going to die!" I said, and now the tears came freely.

He came over and put his arms around me. "Tommy, I'm so sorry. I knew he was ill. Was it what you suspected?"

"Yes!"

"Well, maybe there's still hope. You know, today with everything—"

"No, Don, it's terminal! They said about six or eight months at the most."

"Maybe it's best, Tom. At least he won't have to suffer so much."

"Yes, I suppose you're right. I know what's coming, and yet I can't face it! I've never really had anyone that close to me die before. I feel lost, in a way!"

"I know! But you'll come through it. You've a good head and know where it's at and what you must do; I don't have to tell you."

Of course, he was right, and I knew it, but just having the comfort of a friend at a time when I needed it so desperately made me feel a little better as I walked home later that evening.

The following Sunday I went for dinner at my parents'. My dad asked me to shave him, and when I was finished I told him that I was going to Miami on an orientation the following Wednesday but would be back on Sunday and would see him then. He told me to have a good time, but I explained that it would be mostly work and little fun. We talked and joked for a while, and then I left for home. The next day, I made arrangements to have Dad sent to Calvary Hospital in the Bronx because I felt he would get better care there than he could at home. They had planned to admit him on Friday.

Wednesday, along with a full plane of travel agents, I left for Miami Beach. We were booked at the Sans Souci Hotel and were assigned roommates. Fortunately, mine was gay, so it made things a bit easier for me—although I wasn't interested in him. We made the usual rounds—dinner at one hotel, breakfast at another, and a show somewhere else. For two days it was rush rush, and I was beginning to get bored. On Friday, there was a semiformal dinner-dance we were supposed to attend, but I had no intentions of going. About 5:15 I had my hair cut in the barbershop of the hotel, and as I was leaving, ran into a girl with whom I worked at the agency. She just had had her hair done for the dance and asked how I liked it.

"It's lovely!" I said. "But I'm not going."

We chatted for a while, and then I left her and returned to my room. I finished showering and shaving when Bill, my roommate, came in with a friend, and they made themselves drinks. They asked if I wanted one, and I said no, that I was going to dinner soon then perhaps to a bar.

I was in the bathroom when the phone rang and Bill answered it. "Tom, it's for you!" he said.

I couldn't imagine who would be calling, and when I picked up the phone, I heard, "Mr. Devlin? Long-distance calling."

"Thomas?" It was Mary's voice, and I knew something had happened. "You better come home. Daddy died!"

I heard the words but couldn't believe them. *They told me six or eight months,* I said to myself. *It's only been a week and a half, it couldn't be—not yet!* then to the phone, "When?"

"Six-fifteen! Mom had just returned from the hospital. They took him there this afternoon, and she had just come in when the hospital called. It was twenty-four-hour pneumonia."

"How's Mom taking it?"

"Very well, surprisingly enough. She's holding up very well. But try to get back tonight!"

"All right! Don't do anything till I call. I'll make all the arrangements when I get to New York. I'll call the airlines and explain the situation."

We hung up, and Bill and his friend, who naturally had heard the conversation, looked at me.

"Your dad?" he said.

I nodded and then excused myself and went into the bathroom, locked the door, and cried until there were no tears left.

A few minutes later, Bill knocked at the door. "You okay, Tom? Anything I can do?"

I opened the door, thanked him, and apologized. His friend, out of courtesy, had left, and Bill suggested we go for a drink—that it might help. I agreed, but first I had to try to get a flight back to New York. I called National Airlines and explained the situation. They called back within twenty minutes and told me I was on their 10:00 P.M. flight. It was now about 7:45 P.M. I packed my things, and Bill and I went downstairs to the bar. We sat most of the time in silence, and he tried to cheer me up, but my mind was on what I had to do when I reached New York. After three drinks we left. I said good-bye and took a cab to the airport. I called Joe in New York and told him what had happened and asked if he would pick me up at the airport. He said he would be waiting.

I had tried at the beginning of the month to stop smoking and was doing very well, but on the flight home I smoked almost a full pack. Now I was nervous and had several drinks as well.

Joe met me at the airport and drove me home. We talked little, and when we reached the apartment, George was surprised to see me.

"I didn't expect you till Sunday," he said. "How come you're home so soon?"

"My dad died tonight!"

He told me how sorry he was and made some drinks for Joe and me while I called my mother. My brother answered the phone. He and his wife had arrived earlier.

"How's everything?" I asked.

"Fine. Everyone's here!"

"Okay. Ask Linda [my sister-in-law] to pick me up at 10:00 A.M. in the morning. We have to go to the hospital first."

We talked a bit longer, then hung up. Joe said it was late and had to leave. I thanked him for picking me up and told him I would call him when the funeral was over.

Next morning after I received the death certificate, I spoke with the nun in charge. She did all the arranging for me because I really didn't know what to do. It was now Saturday afternoon. From there we went to the funeral home, where I selected a casket. They said my dad wouldn't be ready for viewing until Sunday evening. I had hoped to have him buried on Monday and avoid the long wake period, but couldn't have a mass said for him until Wednesday.

I arrived at the funeral home before my family on Sunday evening. My aunt and cousin were already there. When I walked to the casket and saw my father, I burst into tears, got up, and tried to compose myself. I didn't want my mother to see me like this. I was talking with my aunt and cousin when she and the rest of my family arrived ten minutes later. For three nights we went to the funeral home. Many friends came to pay their respects. On Wednesday morning we had the mass said and then proceeded to Saint Raymond's for the burial. When it was over we returned to my mother's apartment, and I started acknowledging the mass cards we had received. We had lunch, and I stayed until late in the evening.

On the way home, I once again called Don and went over to see him. This time I was composed, and we chatted at length for some time.

"You see, Tom, I was right! You did come through it all right."

"Yes, I guess I did—and Don, thanks for being so understanding!"

He smiled, and we talked further, and since I had gotten little sleep the last four days, I left and went home.

EIGHTEEN

Before we knew how ill my father was, I had planned to take my mother home to her native Ireland and also visit my father's relatives in England. My grandmother in England had died in January at the age of ninety-one, but the rest of my father's family were alive, and I wanted to meet them. This had been scheduled for the end of May. Now, with his passing I changed it to the beginning of September. I thought it would do a world of good for my mother to try and forget the unpleasant ordeal through which we had gone. She had never been on a plane and was nervous about flying. "Let's take a boat!" she said one evening.

"A boat! Mom, if we take a boat, it's five days over and five back. I'll have to leave as soon as I get there. I only have two weeks, you know."

So, it was settled; she'd fly—although she wasn't too thrilled about the thought!

Through my travel agency connections, I booked a charter flight, which was cheaper. After we boarded the plane and had taken off, she said to me, "I think I know that man in front of us. He used to live on our block years ago. Although I haven't seen his face yet, his voice is familiar!"

Sure enough, she knew him, and they talked for hours. Here I was worried how she would take a flight, and she wasn't bothered one bit—in fact, she loved it!

We arrived at Shannon Airport too late to catch the last flight to Dublin, where my aunt was to meet us. My mother was upset now and began to cry when a flight attendant came to us and said, "Your sister knows you missed the flight. We told her you would be coming by bus, and she will meet you at the Dublin airport accordingly!"

I thanked her and told my mother everything would be okay.

Five hours later, we arrived in Dublin. I was exhausted! Five hours on the plane, a time loss of another five hours, now five more hours on a bus. When my mother saw her sister, they ran to each other and cried like babies. I beamed with happiness! They hadn't seen each other in almost forty years.

We drove to her sister's house and had something to eat. Then my uncle suggested we go to the pub for a drink. Tired as I was, we all agreed.

I met my cousins, uncles, and grandmother who was eighty-three now and a bit senile, which was to be expected.

We stayed a week in Ireland then flew to London for two nights, did some sightseeing, then took a train to Cumberland, where my father's people lived.

There, I had so many uncles and cousins, I couldn't count them. We had a wonderful time, and when we were leaving, my aunt, who was also my godmother since she was in America when I was born, said, "It's wonderful seeing you both again! I wish you would come back soon. I feel this is the last time we'll see one another."

I told her we would try, but, unfortunately we didn't and she passed away a few years later. We stayed in Ireland another four days then flew back to America.

A week after my return, I met someone outside the park, and after we talked for a while, asked him to my apartment. George was at his mother's, although I didn't know it and expected him at any moment. My "friend" and I didn't get along, and I suggested we postpone our activities for another night. As I walked him to the door, I looked in the mirror at the entrance in time to see his arm go around my neck. He dragged me across the room, and with the cord of an old vacuum cleaner, tied my hands behind my back and demanded money. I told him I had none, having just returned from vacation—which was true. He took my watch, ten dollars, and my tape recorder. From my position on the floor, scared out of my wits but trying to avert any more trouble, I said, "Would you mind leaving me a dollar so I can get to work? It's all I have!"

To my surprise he left the dollar, and then as he was leaving with the recorder, said, "Don't call the cops. If you do, I'll tell them we had pot. I hid some while you were in the bathroom."

"Don't worry," I said, "I won't! Just take what you want and leave me alone!"

When he left, I got up and walked backwards to the door. Reaching up I managed to lock it and said out loud, "There! You won't be back for a second load, and the recorder's not working."

Somehow I managed to get out of the cord and went over to my little bar and made a stiff drink. Still shaking, I phoned everyone I knew to tell them what had happened. I got the same response from everyone: "Are you all right? Did he hurt you?"

"No, I'm fine!"

"Good! Then let me get back to sleep. I'll talk with you tomorrow!"

After I made the calls, I looked at the clock. Two-thirty A.M. No wonder they were upset. Oh, well!

I met a boy named Vinny, and we started seeing one another on a regular basis. In November, Bill and I once again went to San Juan. Either I was getting bored with the place or there wasn't anything available because we didn't meet too many people. When I returned home, Bobby Garcia and Vinny picked us up at the airport, drove Bill home and then me. I couldn't wait to get Vinny in bed, after which he didn't call too often. I suppose I was a bit rough that evening. C'est la vie!

New Year's Eve 1968–69 was once again spent at our apartment. There were not as many people as the years before, but it was still pleasant.

I was working in Forest Hills part-time for the same travel agency (they had four offices throughout the city), and in May an orientation to Mexico for ten days was offered to us, which I accepted, and we were to leave on May 5. I arranged my vacation from my night job to coincide with the Mexico trip.

Since May 3 was the first anniversary of my father's death, I went to visit his grave. I had, weeks before, ordered a headstone because I couldn't afford one at the time he passed away. When I arrived, his grave was easily found. It was the only one in the line without a headstone and I was very upset. After I left the cemetery, I phoned the company from which I had ordered the headstone and told them that if it wasn't in by the end of the week, I was canceling my order. Of course, by the end of the week I would be in Mexico, but I had to tell them something to get action.

We left Wednesday for our ten-day tour of Mexico. We arrived in Mexico City and spent one night there. Next morning, bright and early we were up, breakfasted, and off to another town; then another, then another. This was to be our schedule for the entire time. We returned to Mexico City and saw the ballet and bullfights, then off to Taxco for the day; then Acapulco and home. In Acapulco, we were more or less "on our own." We took a boat ride, and with the beautiful Latin music the orchestra was playing, I asked one of the older women to dance. She accepted, and we danced beautifully together. Before long, I had most of the women on our tour lined up, waiting to dance with me. It made me feel great, but I would have preferred it had they been men. Dream on, Tom, dream on!

When we returned to New York, I felt more tired then before I went away. In ten days I had seen more of Mexico than the average tourist would see in three weeks, what with the heavy, hectic schedule we were on.

Stan invited me to his house for Memorial Day. There I met a boy named Jerry, who was the older brother of Allan, whom I had met the year before. Suffice it to say, he was, being more experienced, much more sexually interesting than his younger brother. The weekend passed quickly, and once again I was back at work.

For weeks I had been going to a bar in the Village called the Stonewall Inn. On June 27, the police raided it, and the gay community fought back. Fortunately for me, I wasn't there that particular night. This was to be the beginning of the gay liberation movement. The pictures in the paper were terrible, with one poor man impaled on a fence in his effort to escape. This would last for three days, and the last Sunday in June there is always a big parade for what is now called Gay Pride Day, and the week prior to that is called Gay Pride Week. A fabulous and exciting affair.

The first week in November, Bill and I flew again to San Juan. We had a much better time than the year before. However, the hotel at which we were staying was in the process of renovations: dust all over the place, workmen passing our windows every morning and drilling, hammering, and banging from 7:30 A.M. until 5 P.M. One afternoon we returned from the beach and decided to order drinks and sit on the terrace. When we walked to the window, the terrace was gone. They had removed it while we were at the beach. In its place was a long platform running the entire length of the building.

After showering we ordered drinks in our room. As we both knew we could easily have two, we ordered two. As I sipped mine, I tasted something strange and said to Bill, who was writing cards, "There's something strange in this glass! It tastes like ground glass."

"Don't be silly, Tommy, it must be the sugar! Just hasn't melted yet!"

"No, taste it!"

He did and felt the same thing I did. He took it out of his mouth, and sure enough—ground glass! Somehow the open-air bar was directly in the path of the workmen, and some glass must have fallen down and gotten into the mixer. I called and complained, but all they would do is refresh our drinks at no charge. I asked to speak to the manager but was told he wasn't around. I made a mental note to write him as soon as I returned home. I did write him, and he didn't have the courtesy to acknowledge my letter. Whenever I booked hotels in San Juan from that point on, I made sure my customers did not stay at that hotel.

A few weeks before Christmas, I met a very handsome boy in a bar, whose name was Richard and lived in Queens. Again, Italian and very good-looking! We called each other, and on Christmas night, after work, he asked me to come out. He gave me a bottle of the Baron cologne, which I loved, and I spent the night. It was wonderful! Next day I went to my mother's for dinner.

We celebrated New Year's Eve 1969–70 in our apartment once again.

One evening in January, I invited Richard for dinner; we both were dessert, and it was fabulous. The following week he called and told me he had met someone and was now going steady. *That's fast!* I thought.

Although I didn't believe him, I didn't pursue the matter further and wished him luck and told him to keep in touch from time to time. He never did!

Bill Bushe had now been seeing a boy named Ralph for some time. One evening we had dinner, and after I left them I decided to go for a drink since it was only ten o'clock. At the bar I noticed an extremely handsome young Puerto Rican giving me the eye. At first I thought he might be looking at someone behind me and turned to see who it might be. There was no one behind me! I smiled and went over to him. His name was Tony Morales, and after some conversation we went to my apartment.

The following night when I returned from work, I was surprised to see him in my apartment talking with George. George, thinking I had a date with him, naturally let him in to wait for me. I was pleased to see him, and we started seeing each other after that. A few weeks later I felt I didn't want to be tied down and told him. He seemed upset, and I tried to fix him up with some friends I thought would be interested in his particular type, but he didn't seem to be interested in any of them. So I just let it ride and still saw other people. The middle of June, he told me he was going into the service. We said our farewells, and he was off.

In July I decided to take a long trip. I flew to Los Angeles with David. I stayed with Bobby Lanza, my old flame, and the lover for whom he had left me years before. Bobby Garcia joined us the following day. We took in the sights, took pictures, and the following Monday I took off for Hawaii—my first time there, and I was looking forward to it very much. Although I was alone, I stayed at the Hilton Hawaiian Village and had a good time.

I took a sight-seeing bus tour, and although it was enjoyable, I was a bit restless. I didn't know if there were any gay bars, and if there were, I didn't know where they were. One afternoon I was lying on the beach and decided to do some sightseeing on my own. After I had showered and changed, I rented a car and began my tour of the island. I drove for about an hour, took pictures, and stopped for something to eat. When I got back on the highway, somehow I made a wrong turn and got lost. I asked directions several times and finally found myself approaching downtown Honolulu during the height of the rush-hour traffic. Just like home! An hour later I pulled into the garage at the hotel. As I was returning across the grounds, I had to make a detour because a film company was shooting *Hawaii Five-O*. I stopped and watched for several minutes then went to my room.

Two days later, I left for Tahiti. It was a long flight—seven hours—and it was evening when I arrived. I had made arrangements to have a guide meet me at the airport and drive me to the hotel. When we met, he presented me with a lei—my first in Tahiti! His name was Louis, and he was very nice—and also gay! He told me the hotel I had originally booked was completely filled for the night, so I was put up at another hotel. As we drove along the road, he ran into a friend of his who was on a bicycle. He introduced us, and Roberto got into the stationwagon after putting his bicycle in the rear. We went to the hotel, and Louis told me that Roberto would "show me the town" after I changed. The hotel was beautiful and had a small patio that overlooked its grounds.

When I finished dressing, Roberto took me to the hotel I had booked originally to see the show. It was lovely! After it was over, the lead dancer joined us since he was a friend of Roberto's. We were introduced, and he asked me in perfect English, "Do you speak French?"

"No!"

"Tahitian?"

"No, I'm sorry—just English," I said, trying to be friendly.

"Too bad!" he answered then turned his back and continued talking with Roberto and the others who had joined us. If looks could kill, he'd have been dead on the spot. I felt completely lost and wanted to leave. *These people are very ill-mannered,* I thought to myself. *He can speak English as well as I can. How fuckin' rude!*

I interrupted the conversation and told Roberto I was going back to the hotel and asked where I might get a taxi. He said he would go with me. He did and spent the night with me. It turned out to be a very enjoyable evening, and I was looking forward to four more days in this glorious place.

The following night we went to see another show, after which Roberto took me to a bar in the main section of Papeete. It was called Whisky-A-Go-Go, and it was a very dark bar crowded with men. The dance floor, however, had straight couples dancing rock 'n' roll, which I didn't like anyway. After Roberto excused himself, he went to talk with some friends and left me seated at the bar, alone. I didn't speak the language and again felt lost. A few people made attempts at conversation, but we couldn't relate. I looked at one point to see Roberto leave, and I was really alone. A gentleman seated next to me in a suit asked me the same questions as the dancer had the night before. I naturally gave the same answers to which he replied, "Pity!"

I was so pissed that I finished my drink and decided to call a cab.

The driver of the taxi we had taken earlier was outside the bar when I came out. He motioned to me and asked if I was returning to the hotel. *How fast they speak English when it comes to money,* I thought. I told him I was, and he asked me to sit up front with him and talk while he drove. I thought nothing of it. He was heavy-set and older, and I certainly wasn't interested. When we arrived at the driveway of the hotel, I handed him five francs, which was equivalent to five dollars in American money. The fare was three francs, and tipping was prohibited. He gave me two francs back, and as I was putting them in my shirt pocket, he took my hand to his privates and wanted me to carry on with him. I told him no and started to leave the car, but not before he attempted to take the money out of my shirt pocket. I told him I didn't do those things and left the car. Next day I told Louis about what had happened, and he couldn't believe it.

"What can I say, Tom? Usually my people aren't like this!" he explained.

"Oh, I wasn't upset, just annoyed! If he had been nice looking, well, maybe it would have been another story." I smiled at him.

That afternoon, along with two middle-aged women from the Midwest, we went on a car sightseeing tour of the island, had lunch, and stopped at a black sand beach for about an hour. The island was truly beautiful and an ideal spot for honeymooners. Since I was not on a honeymoon, I couldn't wait to leave.

The following morning I had made arrangements to visit Mooréa, an hour and a half by boat from Tahiti. I arrived early and wanted to have something to eat and went to a small cafe near the boat dock.

"Just coffee and a danish, please," I asked the heavy-set French woman behind the counter.

"Only French pastry!" she growled-back with a nasty attitude.

I looked at the display. Everything they had contained cream and looked so fattening, especially at 8:30 in the morning. I tried to explain what I wanted, but she didn't seem to understand—or want to understand! Finally, I asked her if she spoke English.

"Only French!" she snapped back and walked away from me. *If she could only speak French, how did she know what I said?* I thought, *these people have got to be the nastiest I've ever come up against. They don't even TRY to understand you.* I settled for one of their gooey pastries, had coffee, and left thinking I could make up for it at lunch on Mooréa.

The boat ride across was very long and the waters very choppy. I didn't know anyone on board as my guide wasn't traveling with me. This was supposed to be for the day, and we were to return back to Tahiti about 5 P.M. that afternoon. We arrived and went to the Bali Hai hotel, where we were to have lunch. The owners, who were American, upon learning that I was a travel agent, took me on a short tour of the premises, which were really very lovely, again perfect for honeymooners. We then had lunch, and when they brought mine, it consisted of lobster—which I don't like. There were no substitutes, and all I had was a bit of salad and the carrots. Then off on a sightseeing tour of the island with two older men. We traveled for about three hours, stopping at copra plantations and the Gauguin Museum with all its lovely paintings. When we arrived back at the dock, we were in time to see the boat leaving for Tahiti. There was no alternative but to fly back, so the two men and I took a plane, the cost of which was $3.75, and we were back in Tahiti in twelve minutes.

When I got to the hotel, I was starved! I knew better than to order room service because I would have to wait for hours. Tahitians cannot be hurried, as I had found out. I went to the restaurant in the hotel. It was now sunset, and I was the only customer. I ordered a hamburger and coffee and waited almost an hour. I thought I would faint from the hunger! When it arrived I gulped it down and went back to my room, showered, changed, and made reservations for dinner and the show.

Monday morning I left for Los Angeles and San Francisco, where Bobby was to join me. We missed each other after I had gone through customs in Los Angeles, and we met at the San Francisco airport. I was surprised that Jim (my next-door neighbor from Ninetieth Street) and Terry showed up to meet us. We drove into town in Jim's car, and I told Terry I would call him the next day.

After being in warm climates for over a week, the nights in San Francisco were cold, and I hadn't brought warm clothes with me. Bobby and I were freezing every night. Terry came over and took us on a sightseeing tour. I hadn't seen him in years, and he looked fabulous. We joked and drove for hours. The following day, Jim took us to Carmel and Monterey for the day.

We had lunch at Big Sur and all in all had a great time. In the evening Bobby and I went to the bars and one afternoon took in the baths. The following Sunday we took the plane back to New York.

I met Bill Lopez's nephew, and we spent the night together. I saw him a few times after that, and Bill jokingly asked if I were doing a number on the Lopez family. I told him that his nephew was very nice, but there was nothing permanent about our relationship.

Halloween we went to a friend's house and then to the bars. I wore my Grable outfit again, and at the time was seeing another boy I had met recently. He wanted to go for coffee after we left the bar, and I wasn't up to coffee. I told him I wanted to go home and get out of the outfit, then I would have coffee with him—or better still, we'd have it when we got to my apartment. He was annoyed and after he changed his costume, left. And so, another trick bit the dust, so to speak!

The first week in November, Bill and I again went to San Juan, which now seemed like a second home. As in the past, we saw Jorge, and from time to time he and I got together.

One afternoon after we had returned from the beach and had both showered and shaved for the night, I set my hair in the front in about three or four rollers. We were having drinks when we heard a loud bang. Forgetting about the hair and with towels around our waists, Bill and I opened our door, which faced the open-air lobby. We looked down in time to see the tire of a car come rolling across the street and into the lobby. By this time other guests had come onto the balcony as well. Then it dawned on me that my hair was in rollers, but times have changed. I was so embarrassed, but what the hell!

After our return I heard from Tony. He told me he was coming to New York for a few days and then was leaving for overseas, where he would be stationed for about eighteen months. At this point I had learned to care for him very much.

He had been writing to me, and I answered all his letters. He would occasionally call, and I was getting deeper and deeper into a situation I really didn't want but didn't realize it.

When he returned, we were together every day. The night before he was to leave for San Francisco and overseas, Ray Zimmer had a party. We laughed and joked for hours and then left. As we were driving home, Tony started to cry, and I thought it was because he was leaving and asked what was wrong, but he didn't answer. The following morning, I drove him to the airport and told him not to look back as he was going through the gate to his plane. I watched him and all of a sudden had a lost feeling. Was I in love with him? It certainly seemed that way! I didn't want to, but already I began to miss him.

That afternoon, I called Ray to thank him for the party. During our conversation, he said to me, "Your friend Tony is very nice, Tommy, but if I were you, I'd watch him!"

"What do you mean?" I asked, not knowing what he was talking about.

"Well, remember when you went to the bathroom and saw Tony in there?"

"Yes, what about it?"

"Well, my friend Terry told me that he was carrying on with Tony when you knocked on the door. When they heard it was you, Terry jumped in the shower and pulled the curtain. That's why you didn't see him when you came in."

"Oh, I see! Good thing I didn't, either. I'd have pulled her blonde hair out by its black roots!" I said, and I was angry now—angry not only at Tony but at what an idiot I must have seemed. No wonder he was crying in the car on the way home; he felt guilty!

I thanked Ray for the information and again for the nice time we had had, and told him I would watch out for Tony from here on in. Later in the evening, Tony called from San Francisco, and I informed him of what I had learned.

"I know, Tommy, and I'm sorry. It won't happen again, I promise!"

"Better not. Why do you have to fool around when you have someone? I don't understand you!"

"I don't understand me, either," he said.

We talked a bit longer and then hung up. Yes, I cared about him! I was in love, and the thought of him with someone else upset me very much, but what could I do? It was over and done with, so I'd best forget it.

New Year's Eve 1970–71. It was almost a ritual now: the party was held at our apartment. It was more crowded than some of the years before, but everyone seemed to be enjoying themselves, as usual.

Shortly after midnight the phone rang, and it was Tony calling—collect—from Okinawa! I was very happy he thought of me, and it made the evening even better. Again, it seemed as though I had a lover—I didn't expect him to be faithful, nor did he expect me to be. After all, he was halfway around the world, so there was no choice but to enjoy whatever came along.

NINETEEN

Once again, George decided he wanted to live alone and moved to West End Avenue, and again I had a place to myself. I missed him, of course, but there are times in which we all want to be by ourselves and I had no objections.

Cliff Wayne, who had come to my Stars of the '40s party, was well on his way to stardom. He had appeared on several TV shows and was due for a concert at Carnegie Hall. Along with Helenmae, Connie, Joe, George, and several other friends, we went to see him. We had excellent box seats, and I felt so proud as he entertained and held his audience. Here was someone I knew and loved so well, on stage in front of a capacity audience and being received so well.

Backstage after the performance, his dressing room was crowded with celebrities. When he came out and saw me, he nodded in recognition. We had, of course, spoken on the phone many times during the week and earlier that day. When I finally made my way to him, we spoke softly for a few minutes, and he introduced me to his family. Then he grabbed me and took me into his dressing room along with George.

"How the hell do I get out of here, Tommy? There's so many people!"

"I don't know, Cliff! But that's the price you have to pay for being a star now!" I said, smiling. He laughed, and we returned to the outer room, spoke a while longer, and then I told him, "Look, I know you've a party to go to now, but if you can get away later, Helenmae is having a party at George's apartment.

I gave him the address, and he said he would try, but we shouldn't count on it. Needless to say, he didn't make the party.

Before Cliff left the city he again called me to say good-bye. He said he would keep in touch, but that he had little time for writing and asked me to try to understand. I told him I fully understood.

In September, Bill and I went to Provincetown for the weekend. I hadn't been there in such a long time, it was like a new experience for me. Don Venta had secured reservations for us across the street from where he had a part-interest in a building along with a friend. We saw much of him during our stay. The day we were leaving, Bill decided to take the bus back with me and keep me company rather than fly as he had intended; he had flown up and I had taken the bus. We had a sandwich before we left, and he suggested taking something on the bus to eat on our way home.

"That's not necessary, Bill. They made a stop coming up, and I'm sure they'll stop in Providence on the way home."

We boarded the bus and started for New York. It didn't stop in Providence, or anywhere else for that matter and we were starved. Across the aisle from us, a woman took out some fried chicken and began eating. We both looked at her and then at each other, and our tongues almost hit the floor. The ride seemed endless, and when we reached New York, Bill said, "Never again! That's it for buses!"

"Me, too! Next time, we'll fly as we usually do. I've had it, too. Can't wait to get home and hit the fridge—that is, if I have anything in it." I should have known better after the Washington incident years ago.

October for Halloween, I had my professional makeup man come, and with George's expertise on the red wig, went to several bars. I wore a black turtleneck leotard, short fringe skirt, and feather boa. One bar we went to was Spanish, and under the soft lights the makeup was sensational. Later, we made the rounds and returned home quite high.

In November Bill and I were back to San Juan, this time staying at a converted condominium. The apartment was lovely, but we were only on the fourth floor, and the noise from the street was impossible, even with the windows closed.

One day we returned from the beach early to see a man in the kitchen by the refrigerator and asked what he was doing.

"Someone reported the light was out and I'm putting in a new bulb," he said and left.

We couldn't imagine why anyone would report a lightbulb, and Bill and I just looked at each other.

"I don't believe it, Tommy," he said. "Something's wrong!"

We looked in the refrigerator, and I noticed that the bottle of rum I had in there was half empty.

"I know what it is," I said. "He's been sucking up on my rum. Can you beat that?"

"Figures—they'll smell it out!" He smiled.

Not that the rum was expensive, but I wanted to know it was there whenever I wanted a drink, so I decided to find another place for my liquor.

On December 5 another friend named Tony and I saw *Hello Dolly* with Ethel Merman. We had gotten the tickets from a friend of Bobby Garcia who was doing the hair for the show. We had excellent seats and enjoyed it very much.

Christmas Eve I was invited to a party where I ran into several old friends. At the end of the evening, I asked two of them to my apartment for drinks. One thing led to another, and the three of us had sex. It was great! The Japanese boy left, and the Puerto Rican spent the night. At this point in my life, what else was new?

New Year's Eve of 1971–72 went along as usual, and during the evening I asked Bobby Garcia what had happened to another mutual friend, by the name of Sonny. He was never late, and we began to worry. He hadn't called, and as the evening wore on, we had assumed he had met someone and didn't get around to calling.

The following afternoon, Bobby called me, in tears. "Tommy, Sonny's dead!"

"Dead! That's impossible! We just saw him last week. What happened?"

"I don't know the full story, but from what I understand he went to a restaurant out here [New Jersey] New Year's Eve around eight or nine o'clock, and there was a robbery, and he was shot in the leg and head. He lived almost a day."

"Oh, my God! That's terrible!" I said.

"The funeral is tomorrow. Can you come?"

"Of course!"

He gave me the information, and the following day I took a bus to the funeral home in New Jersey. After we paid our respects, we went to the crematorium and then to Bobby's apartment. It had been snowing very heavily the night before and all day, and the afternoon seemed to drag by. Finally everyone seemed to perk up a bit, and about 7:00 P.M. I returned to Manhattan.

In February I ran into a friend I hadn't seen in many years. We talked for some time, and he told me he was looking to share an apartment with someone on a temporary basis. Thinking it was just that—temporary—I told him he could stay with me. When he moved in, he had two little dogs and so much furniture, the apartment looked like a warehouse, and I was furious.

George and I saw *Follies* in March and enjoyed it very much. In May, Bobby, my roommate, whose name was also Tony, and I drove to Providence, Rhode Island for the weekend. We stayed at a hotel, while Tony visited family. In the evening, we went to one bar that I really liked. It was clean and very neat, and the people we met seemed friendly.

In June Tony Morales returned from overseas with his new lover. He had written me that he was going with someone, and I now had it in my mind that our affair was over. A few days after he arrived, he and his lover stayed overnight. Next day, he told me he wanted to go back with me, and, like a fool, I agreed.

I had had it with my roommate and finally asked him to move. It took him several weeks at a slow pace to remove all his belongings but finally he was gone.

Cliff Wayne was appearing at the Playboy Club in New Jersey for the Fourth of July weekend and asked me to come and stay over since he had a large suite. Unfortunately, I couldn't make it because a few weeks before a bar acquaintance friend of mine who was an excellent portrait artist was working on my portrait, and the last sitting was the Fourth of July. I was disappointed in not seeing Cliff, but he understood.

The end of October, out came the Grable outfit, only with a long, red wig. The makeup again was done by Bill, who, by now, was my "makeup man" on a permanent basis. The bar had a small contest, and I came in second.

About 8:00 A.M. on November 1, my sister Pat called and told me her little boy had died in his sleep. I wasn't fully awake and told her I'd call her back. I hung up and went back to bed. When I lay down it dawned on me what she had said, and I called her back immediately. She said she had woken up early and found him. I called my mother, then Hertz, and rented a car.

I picked Mom up and drove to Long Island and stayed overnight. Since my little nephew was only three and a half years old, the funeral was the following day. As we entered the church and Pat saw the tiny casket, she almost fainted but composed herself, and with my brother on one arm and myself on the other, she entered the church.

When the funeral was over, we returned to Pat's house and had something to eat. This was the second time that someone in my family had died while another member was in Florida. This time my brother-in-law (the baby's father) had been playing with his group in Florida. I gave orders that no one go to Florida as long as Mother was alive. This was a quirk on my part resulting from my having been in Florida when my dad had passed away. This, of course, was ignored and Mary went a few times, and, thank God, nothing happened.

Shortly before Christmas, I was invited to a party in Long Island, and Tony Morales and I attended. During the course of the evening, I found him talking with another boy in the bedroom. Knowing him as well as I did now, I suspected something but said nothing. He informed me they knew each other (don't they always?) from before, and were just talking. I wanted to believe him, so I left them and joined the party.

Christmas Eve we were again invited to a party, and in the morning Tony told me he was going to the Bronx to visit his sister. I reminded him about the party and asked that he be back by at least 8:00 or 9:00 o'clock. When he hadn't returned by 10:30, I was furious and knew right away that he was with the boy to whom he had been talking and at the party in Long Island. I went to the party alone and tried to have a good time. The party was boring, and I returned home about 3:30.

When I woke Christmas morning, Tony still hadn't returned, and I was really fuming. Before I left to have dinner at my mother's, I left Tony a note.

Tony:
Here's your Christmas gift! Be out of my house by the time I get home at 7:30. I'm very upset! You know you were to have dinner with us and didn't even have the decency to call—so that's it, baby!

Tom

When I returned home, he was gone. I felt bad about what

I had done, but I had hoped it would teach him a lesson. So, once again, I was free!

New Year's Eve 1972–73 I gave a small party and a few days before had relented and invited Tony, but he didn't come. I was never the type to stay angry for any length of time.

In early February or March, I met a young boy by the name of Steve Cummings. We weren't interested in one another on a sexual level but enjoyed talking together whenever we saw each other in a bar. We started calling one another and soon became good friends.

On July 3 Betty Grable died of cancer. I knew from the papers she had been ill, but it still came as a shock. My favorite! I received many calls after her death because everyone knew how much I liked and admired her.

One evening in early August, I was in a bar and met a nice-looking Italian boy by the name of Tony Scott. So many Tonys lately! He seemed very sweet, and we talked for some time before I asked him to my apartment. He worked as a waiter in one of the bars and would come over to my apartment usually about four or five in the morning. What I didn't appreciate was the fact that he drank very heavily. I thought I was a drinker, but he had me beat!

The beginning of September, two friends of Tony's got "married" and held the reception at the bar in which Tony worked. Since I was seeing him, I was also invited. Every table was taken, and we had a marvelous afternoon. I liked the two boys, and they seemed very happy together. In a way, I envied them and secretly wished it were me. A few nights later, we were invited to their apartment for a birthday party, and Tony, as usual, arrived late. He began drinking, and later we went to a bar, where he had still more to drink. I finally persuaded him to go home and put him to bed.

I liked Tony, but it was getting to be too much for me. I was getting little sleep because of the hours he kept, and then when he came home and started drinking by the time we went to bed, he'd just pass out. This would continue nightly, and I was becoming quite frustrated.

I was invited to a birthday party by a South American friend, and Bobby and I attended. I met a Spanish boy and invited him home, knowing Tony would be there. When we arrived Tony was being very, very friendly with a boy he said was only a friend. I told him to go right ahead and be friendly while *my* friend and I went into the bedroom. After that, Tony and I decided it would be best to go our separate ways. I felt the breakup would be easier this way—and it was!

Halloween night I was invited to a party and wore my long, red wig, dark green leotard, and a multi-colored, floor-length skirt. We stayed at the party for an hour or so and then hit the bars. Nothing terribly exciting!

A few days later I learned that my doctor had died. He, too, had been ill for some time, and I was saddened by his passing.

The day after Christmas I flew to San Francisco. Bill Lopez and Ken had moved there because Bill's company had transferred him to Palo Alto. Since I had left the travel agency earlier in the year, I had to pay the full fare—and it hurt, even if it was a special excursion.

It was raining very heavily as I boarded the plane at Kennedy Airport, and when I arrived five hours later in San Francisco, I was also greeted by another heavy rain. When I saw Ken, I smiled and said, "I had to leave New York for this?"

After we got my luggage we drove to his apartment. Bill hadn't been feeling well and was at home when we arrived. After the usual greetings, I had something to eat and Ken and I went to a few bars.

They arranged a party in my honor for the following night, and I was introduced to Bill and Ken's friends. It was very pleasant, and I enjoyed myself very much, especially with one of their friends who spent the night with me.

Ken had arranged his vacation so he could spend it with me when he learned I was coming. This was amusing, in a way. Bill was my first lover, and here I was more friendly with his present lover. Such is life!

Ken took me to many places during my stay. We went to a movie one afternoon, into San Francisco for some shopping another time, and to the baths, as well. Ken warned me not to say anything to Bill, which, of course, I didn't.

New Year's Eve of 1973–74 was to be different than other years. We spent it at one of their local bars. It wasn't very crowded, and although I enjoyed being with Bill and Ken, I missed New York and my other friends. I hated being in a bar on New Year's Eve. I hadn't been in one for years, and it seemed strange.

I saw my friends Jim and Terry. Terry had been ill for about six months, but when I saw him he looked the picture of health and I commented on it. Alan, his cousin, had called me and told me he had been ill earlier in the year, and when I mentioned it to Terry, he said, "Oh, you know Alan, always the dramatic one!"

We had lunch one afternoon together and later went to a beer bar—which I didn't care for but had no choice. About an hour later, Terry and his friend left. As we said good-bye, I had a strange feeling. It was a sad feeling for somehow I knew I would never see him again.

Shortly before I was to return home, Ken and I were in a bar talking with some of his friends, when another friend of Ken's came up behind me and gave me a bear hug. He was big and strong, and I didn't feel anything until the next day. I spent the good part of the day in the emergency room of the local hospital, where they had to put a cummerbund around my waist. Fortunately, nothing was broken, just very badly bruised. Now, whenever anyone tries to give me a bear hug, I move away.

A few days later, I tearfully said good-bye to Bill and Ken and returned to New York. I was sorry to leave but also happy to get back home.

TWENTY

In March I met Ray Harwood and John Lawlor. Ray and I had an affair, and it was just that. John and I seemed to hit it off for some time, but there was something lacking, and I couldn't quite figure it out. We then began seeing one another on a friendly basis, and for all practical matters, it seemed much better.

Through mutual friends, I met a young Puerto Rican boy who lived in New Jersey. He was good-looking and terrific, but, alas, only a few times and then—as before—he seemed to disappear. *Pity,* I thought, *and so nice, too! Probably found a lover!*

I had been corresponding with Tony Morales, who was stationed in Texas, had reenlisted in the service, and then was discharged. I was living alone, and he had expressed his desire to come back to New York. I saw no reason why he couldn't be my roommate and share expenses, and I wrote suggesting it. Yes, I was still interested and thought I'd give it one last try. If it worked, fine, if not, that definitely would be the end for us.

He called me as he started by car for New York. When he reached Ohio, he called again. Finally, I received a call at 11:00 P.M. one evening. He was at the Delaware Bridge and had run out of both gas and money and didn't know what to do. I told him to wait there, and I would come down and get him. There was no way I could send money, so I checked the bus schedule and found I had just missed the last bus. The next was at 6:45 the following morning. I got on it and asked the driver to let me off after we went over the bridge. He told me the bus didn't stop there, and after I explained the situation, he agreed to stop. I approached the police station and described Tony and his car and asked if they had seen him. They said they had, and that he was parked in the rear of the police station. I found him asleep in his car with all his little belongings in the backseat and trunk. We had breakfast, got gas, and drove back to New York.

Several weeks later, Tony was seeing a Puerto Rican guy by the name of Willy Martinez. They had met in an East Side bar that we went to, often called Camp David. I usually sat at the beginning of the bar on a stool against the wall, where I could see people coming and going. Tony would stand behind me and cruise over my shoulder. I caught him at it one time and said, "Mary, go in the back and dance! You make me nervous standing behind me like this."

Willy and Tony started seeing each other, and I liked Willy. He was funny and always kept me in hysterics.

On Halloween night, as I started to get myself together, Tony told me he and Willy had broken up and asked me to go with him to Willy's apartment to pick up some things he had left there. I had already put on my false nails and had to keep my hands in my pockets when we arrived at Willy's. There was also a girl friend of Willy's there when we arrived. Small talk was made, and Willy finally said to me, "Okay, Miss Thing, you can take your hands out of your pockets. We know you have false nails on."

I was embarrassed but just smiled and kept my hands where they were. Tony got his belongings, and we returned to the apartment so I could finish dressing. My makeup man came over.

This time I thought I'd be a little more elegant than with the short bathing suits I had been wearing for years, so I bought a black halter-neck evening gown. I wore a floor-length, sheer, black coat completely covered with rhinestones with white fur collar and cuffs, and the short light-blond wig that George did so beautifully.

Before we left the apartment, I put another pair of shoes and the camera we had used to take pictures in a bag and asked Bill to take it to the bar because I knew my feet would be tired in the shoes I was wearing. There were too many of us for one cab, so we had to take two cabs. When we arrived at the bar, I asked Bill where the bag was. He was quite high and had left it in the taxi. I didn't mind the shoes so much, but the camera belonged to Bill Bushe, who had gotten it from his parents as a gift. Oh, well, I bought him another, but the pictures we had taken were gone forever.

In early December I met a boy named Frank Carpola. We got along fairly well, and I was hoping something might come of it. He came over several times a week, and things seemed once again to be going well for me. But again, they faded.

The apartment below me became vacant and I decided to take it since it had a yard and would be nice in the summer. The rent jumped rather high, and I realized that it was one of the biggest mistakes of my life. Earlier in the summer, I had decided to have my apartment completely air-conditioned and bought a large unit for the living room. I had a man come especially to install it, and the cost set me back quite a bit for both. The bedroom also had an air-conditioner, and why I decided to move, I'll never know. The apartment downstairs was also air-conditioned, so I sold both units to the owner. We were to move New Year's day.

New Year's Eve of 1974–75 we gave a small party. Without a doubt, it turned out to be one of the worst parties I had ever given, and I was very disappointed at the small turnout. I ended it early because the following day we were moving. It took Don, Ray, Steve, Frank, Tony, and myself most of the day to get everything downstairs, but we were finally in!

When everyone had left, Tony and I looked around the

apartment. It looked nothing like when the former tenant had it. He had such beautiful things and really had it fixed up nicely. But the move had been made, and although at this point I was sorry, there was nothing that could be done. I would just have to live with it.

A few weeks later, we had the apartment somewhat in shape. One Saturday morning, I was asleep, when the phone rang. It was Alan, Terry's cousin. "I just wanted to let you know, Tommy, that we buried Terry last Thursday. He died of cancer of the colon!"

Again, I couldn't believe it! It was just about a year ago I had seen him, and he looked so well. I was sick thinking about it the rest of the day. So, my feelings were right after all, the sad feeling I had that afternoon when we said good-bye in Palo Alto. Poor Terry!

In February, I met a guy named Kim. I had been in a bar one evening with Steve and had seen him and commented to Steve on how handsome he was. The following evening I was in the bar alone and was on my way to the men's room when someone grabbed me by the arm and said, "Not leaving, are you?"

It was a line, and I knew it—there wasn't an exit in the rear of the bar, and when I turned and saw who it was, I most fainted! It was the guy I had seen the night before when I was with Steve. I couldn't imagine his talking to me. There were so many good-looking people in the bar, I thought, why should he pick me? But I was delighted!

"No, just the men's room!" I said and started toward the back.

While in there, I thought to myself, *Dumb dumb. He spoke to* you, *make the most of it!*

When I returned, he was standing by the jukebox, taking with friends, so I went to his right and stood by a wall. We looked at each other from time to time and smiled. Finally, he walked away from his friends and came over to me.

"I saw you here last night," he said. "Why didn't you stay? What was your big rush to leave?"

"Oh, I was with a friend, and we wanted to hit a few more bars. Besides, I didn't think you were interested."

"Interested!" he said. "If I weren't interested, do you think I'd be here now?"

"No, I suppose not!"

Had I known the night before that he was interested, I would have told Steve, "Ta ta, honey."

We talked for about ten minutes, and he asked me to leave. I was floating on air! He was so good-looking, I couldn't believe I was actually going with him. We saw each other for the next three nights, then it started—on his part, for a change. He was getting very heavy, and although I was interested, for some reason I couldn't explain, he frightened me. He kept talking about us in the lover sense, and I thought this was too quick, that something was wrong! I didn't believe some of the things he said to me, but I thought it best to end it before it went any further, and so, with a heavy heart, we stopped seeing each another.

A few months later he was in a serious auto accident, and I went to see him in the hospital. He looked so bad I almost cried. At first he didn't remember me, but then he came around. When he was released, he left town to recuperate at his family home out of state. I never saw him again.

On March 14, I was in a bar and met a very nice guy and took him back to the apartment. Tony was working until 3:30 in the morning and usually made something to eat when he came in. I slept in the bedroom and he in the living room. About 8:00 in the morning, something woke me. I looked around and saw smoke coming from the kitchen. *What the hell is she cooking now?* I thought to myself.

He wasn't in the kitchen and was sleeping, but the house was covered with smoke. I looked out the window and saw flames coming from the cellar. The boiler was on fire! I woke my friend, and Tony and we dressed as quickly as we could. Tony was in the living room and was yelling, "Tommy, I can't see!"

"What the hell do you want me to do? See for you?" I said, trying to act calm.

I looked all over for my dog, but the smoke was too intense. I opened the door to the yard, and the flames were getting bigger. I thought any minute the boiler would explode. The other tenants and I went into the street, and my friend helped Tony out. The smoke in the hall was so thick that Tony walked right through the glass front door. It was a miracle he didn't cut himself. We waited as the firemen did their best to make the apartment a complete shambles.

When they finally left and we returned to the apartment, I had to hold back the tears. The living room was a mess! They had broken the windows, the air-conditioner was down in the bottom of the yard, there was a hole in the floor through which you could jump, smoke, soot, and water all over the place. My light yellow rug was now black and had glass, oil, and water all over it. I went into the backyard and there was my dog in a corner, nice and safe and shaking. Poor thing, it must have been terrible for him as well. I called my doctor to cancel the appointment I had that afternoon. I had been under his care for high blood pressure, which I developed shortly after Tony returned. I think that should have given me a clue! I also called my mother and told her what had happened and asked if I could bring the dog out to her to take care of for awhile. Tony had his car, and there was no problem getting there.

Before my friend left, he said, "Well, Tommy, this is one night I won't forget very easily!"

What could be said further? We said good-bye, and I

promised to call but didn't. I had too many problems right then. When the owner saw the damages and had them estimated, he told me I had a two choices: to move out temporarily while the renovations were being done, or move completely. I told him I would think it over but had decided I would move if I could find a place. God must have known I wanted something more reasonable, and this was the answer, or so I thought.

We looked at several apartments, but they were either too small or too expensive. Finally we went to an agency and looked at several more apartments. I saw one on East Eighty-ninth Street that seemed nice, although not exactly what I had in mind, but nonetheless I took it. One week to the day, I had the movers in and moved to East Eighty-ninth street.

Shortly after we moved in, Tony and I had a misunderstanding, which resulted in my asking him to find his own place. We looked around, and he took a place on East Eighty-second Street. We hadn't made it as lovers and now we couldn't make it as roommates. We loved each other but only as friends, at this point; and it would remain that way.

George called one afternoon and told me he was having difficulties with his roommate and asked if he could stay with me temporarily. Again, he was coming back. It seemed as if we were long-lost lovers or something, but since we always got along well together, I said all right. Naturally, I enjoyed living alone, but it would help financially, and knowing him as well as I did, I figured it would only be a matter of time before he'd want to be on his own again—and I could not blame him. It's difficult, at times, with a roommate, no matter how well you get along. In June he moved in. Funny how things seem to always work themselves out!

Since Steve Cummings and I had the same birthday, we thought it might be nice to treat one another to a Broadway musical, which we did on June 24. Along with George, we saw *Over There!* with the Andrews Sisters. Then to the bar for a few drinks, after which Steve went go home. He wasn't much of a drinker; at least, not like us.

Well into October, I decided since the bar in which we were now hanging out was having its Halloween party, it was time that I got myself together. With the help of the roommate of a coworker, I had my new gown made. It was bright red, metallic, cut low in the front again in a V shape, with a slit on the right leg up to the thigh. George, as usual did my wig, which was new and shoulder-length blond on blond. I also borrowed a false female chest, which added to the illusion, and when most of my friends saw me, they thought I had outdone myself (for a change). Tony Morales was my escort.

One Sunday evening, I decided to go to the bar to see who and what was around. After ordering a drink, I noticed a very good-looking Puerto Rican seated a few stools away talking with a friend. He looked familiar, but I was sure we never had slept together. All the Latins I'm interested in were very similar in looks. It was obvious that he had had a few drinks too many, and before long he was staring at me and smiling, and I returned his smile. Shortly, we were in conversation, and I asked him to my apartment.

After finishing our lovemaking, I asked him if he knew me, and he said, "Sure. We met about twelve years ago at Raymond's!"

"You're *that* Milton?" I asked, somewhat surprised because the Milton I knew then did not go with men (or, at least, that's what he had said at the time).

"Yes, it's me!"

"Well, I'll say one thing, you look much better now than you did then."

We continued talking, and he spent the night. The following afternoon he left and promised to call me that evening. He kept his word and called, and we began seeing each other for about two weeks. We continued having sex, but he seemed to be growing restless. Sometimes he wouldn't call, and I was getting rather annoyed. He called one afternoon to tell me he had been mugged the morning before as he was going into the beauty salon at which he worked. I couldn't imagine what he would be doing in the salon at 2:30 in the morning. I was later to learn he was taking someone there to have sex when the incident happened. So much for Milton in my life—at least sexually!

New Year's Eve of 1975–76 was spent at Raymond and Harry's apartment on West Twenty-fifth Street. I nevertheless asked Milton to keep up the pretense for the evening, and after the party we would announce that we were not seeing each other sexually. He agreed, and we went to the party. It was snowing quite heavily as we arrived in Tony's car, and fortunately we found a parking spot across the street from where the party was being held.

During the course of the evening, Bill Bushe was dancing with Tony to some Latin music. Being a bit high, he jokingly pushed Tony into the corner saying, "Mary, you can't dance Latin for shit!"

In pushing him, Tony slid into a chair, which he pushed against the wall holding a bookcase on top of which were several ornaments that almost fell.

Raymond, on seeing this, came over and very nicely and politely said to Bill, "Bill, please be a little careful!"

Bill, who was now high, caused a scene and began to leave. As he was waiting for his friend, he turned to me and said, "Tommy, I am right!"

"No, Bill, this time you're wrong!"

With that he turned and left the apartment.

The first Sunday in January, Joe had a cocktail party, which Milton and I attended. Although there was nothing sexual between us anymore, we nevertheless remained friends. It was a very nice affair, and I saw people I hadn't seen in years, which is always a pleasure. In the meantime, Bill and I were not speaking and remained that way for about two weeks.

Tony and his new-roommate, Chip had taken an apartment in the same building I was in so we were seeing a lot of each other; strictly friendship. In February Chip was working at a local bar that had entertainment almost nightly. He called one evening and asked me to accompany him to hear a girl sing whom he though was great. I did, and she was terrific. Her name was Christine, and after the show she joined us. We had a few drinks, and at the end of the evening Chip took her telephone number. In the weeks that followed, we attended many clubs in which Christine sang, which were gay because she, too, was gay.

Early one morning at the Anvil, an after-hours bar, quite high and tired I met Carlos, a handsome Mexican-Indian who was to become the next interest in my life. We came to my apartment, and since it was very early in the morning, George had already left for work. Carlos and I continued seeing each other for about four weeks. He worked in the Village and would meet me after he got off work. Sometimes we went for a few drinks and then home, but we were together, and I was beginning to care for him very much. He drank heavily, and it upset me. One night he didn't call or meet me, and the next morning he called and said he had lost his job and was feeling down in the dumps. I tried to cheer him up, but it didn't seem to help. He disappeared for about a week, and when he called and came back, he cried like a baby.

"Tommy, what's wrong with me? I do love you, and I don't want to lose you, but I'm so mixed-up. Tell me what to do!"

"Carlos—I do care for you very much, you know that, and I'll help you any way I can. Don't worry, something will turn up—it always does!" After that he went to sleep, and I went to work.

A few days later, he told me he was going downtown to take any job that he could get. I didn't have any change, and I knew he didn't have any money—at least I thought he didn't, so I gave him ten dollars. He didn't come home that evening or call. I was worried and very upset.

The beginning of May, my two young nieces made their Communion, and Tony Morales and I rented a car because Tony's car was long since gone. It was old so he sold it. I wasn't feeling very well at the party, and when I got home I called my doctor and told him what I was experiencing.

"Sounds like a textbook case of hepatitis," he said.

True enough, that night I was in the hospital and was there for two weeks. It wasn't as bad as the time I had it twenty-two years earlier, but methods for treatment were different than they had been years before.

One afternoon my doctor came in and, asked "Is there any diabetes in your family?"

"No, not that I know of, why?"

"Because you're spilling over, and I'm going to put you on medications."

I tested my urine every day, and it was negative, so I couldn't understand why he had me on medication, but then I wasn't a doctor. I lost weight and felt great!

In June, there was a bus ride from one of the Village bars to New Hope, Pennsylvania, and Helenmae, Tony, Dick, Don, and I went for the day. I had never been there, and it was a lovely little town. After dinner we boarded the bus for the trip back to New York.

For the Gay Pride that year we had lunch at a Village bar, and I saw Carlos. He was working at the bar, so we didn't have much conversation. He looked so good I wanted to see him, but, like so many before, I didn't.

My friends were telling me that my hair was beginning to get very grey, and although I liked the silvery look, I decided to change it once again and made it a very ash blonde.

The Fourth of July the "us" crowd got together at Eric's

West Side apartment overlooking the Hudson River to watch the ships for the Bicentennial. It was a lovely afternoon, and the ships were a sight to see.

I called Bill Lopez in Palo Alto and Stan in Dallas, and both were surprised and happy to hear from me. Ken wasn't home, and Bill said that he would be terribly upset to know I had called and that he had missed me.

The first Tuesday in September, Helenmae, my mother, and I took off for Atlantic City. Of course, both Helenmae and I had been there often, but it was Mom's first time. We arrived in the early evening and took two motel rooms in Absecon, one room for Helenmae and Mom and the other for myself. After changing, we drove into Atlantic City for dinner and ate at a rather expensive restaurant, but the food was well worth it. After dinner, we decided that since it was a bit late we wouldn't show Mom any of the town that that night and returned to the motel. The next afternoon I spent sitting by the pool. We were the only guests since it was after Labor Day and the crowds had left. After dinner that night we walked on the boardwalk for awhile then sat on a bench and watched the people go by. This was our routine for the next two nights: not exactly exciting, it was different! I was still on my recovery and only had two very light drinks with dinner and didn't want to take the car into Atlantic City to go to the bars. I just didn't feel right. On Friday, we checked out and drove to visit a friend of my mother's who was now living in New Jersey. We had lunch and later in the evening returned to New York.

TWENTY-ONE

Halloween was once again upon us, and I took the red gown and changed the top to a halter, made a floor-length green theater coat, and bought a new shoulder-length wig, and Bobby Garcia in one of my outfits, his friend David, and I went to a bar in New Jersey. It was a fun evening, and we posed for many pictures. On Halloween itself, I borrowed a solid brown designer dress from a friend and also a red feather boa and went to one of the local bars. In November, I made a powder blue evening gown for Tony Morales and again in my red halter dress and red feather boa, we hit the bars and were later invited to a party by two lovers named Armando and Andy.

The weeks flew by, and once again New Year's Eve was upon us. It was now 1976–77, and the usual bottle party took place, this time at the apartment of Armando and Andy, whom we had met a few weeks before. We had thought we would have about forty people, and during the course of the evening about eighty or ninety showed up. Not all at once, of course, but the apartment was very large, and it didn't seem as though there were that many people. It was one of the best we had had in some time. No drunks, no breakage, no trouble of any kind. People were beautiful!

In January, George once again moved to his own apartment in the is same building in which Helenmae and Joe lived. In February I took an apartment back on the West Side between Columbus and Amsterdam on Eighty-fifth Street with Tony Morales. We seemed to be getting along well, and the months passed quickly. No love affairs to speak of, just one- or two-nighters. On July 13, while I was at work, the city had another blackout. We were fortunate enough to get out of the building in less than an hour and managed to get a taxi, which, in itself, was something! Later that evening after a candlelit dinner (who had a choice?), Tony and I went to a bar and ran into someone I was sort of seeing for a few weeks. We all sat around in the candlelit bar, sang songs, and let the evening slip by.

A few nights later, as I was entering another bar that was fast becoming a favorite, I noticed that the lights were out. I ordered a drink and asked the bartender had what happened.

"Oh, something to do with overloading. It'll be fixed soon!" he answered.

As I was sitting talking with friends, I saw a handsome young Italian talking with the owner. They were close enough that I could hear their conversation. It was generally concerning the lights. *God, he's gorgeous!* I thought to myself. *What a beauty!* At that moment, he looked my way, and we just smiled at one another. This would go on for weeks.

During this time, I was very friendly with another bar acquaintance, by the name of Tom Skouris, an actor of Greek-American descent. We would see each other every week in the bar, and I jokingly said one night that I would get him in bed, and he just laughed. We were to become very close and dear friends.

Weeks later, during which the usual smiles would pass between the Italian and myself, I finally got the nerve to speak to him. I made some comment about the lighting conversation he had had with the owner several days before. It was stupid on my part, but it broke the ice. His name was Jimmy DeVito.

Every time I would go to the bar, I would stop and speak with Jimmy. He was very polite and courteous. Toward the end of August, we were talking one night and he mentioned he was going on vacation to Philadelphia, his hometown. I mentioned

I was also going away but hadn't decided whether to go to Atlantic City or Provincetown since I hadn't been on vacation in either place for some time. During the course of our conversation, I let it be known how much I cared for him, and to my amazement learned that he cared for me as well. I couldn't believe it! Here was a beauty who wanted me as much as I wanted him. *Just like Kim,* I thought. There would be many conversations in the weeks to follow, but at the time I didn't know it.

After Jimmy left on vacation, Tony Morales and I rented a car the day after Labor Day and drove to the Cape. We stayed at a gay guest house in separate rooms and in general had a ball for the week we were there. Even though I had sex with several people, I couldn't wait to get back and see Jimmy. He was on my mind all the time, although, at this point, he and I had not had sex.

Upon my return, I called Jimmy, and he told me he wanted to see me because he had something important to tell me. Needless to say, I almost guessed the reason, and, as it turned out, I was right. He thought he was in love with someone who was not in love with him, and who didn't even know Jim cared. What a mess! At this point I cared so much that it hurt and decided to try and hold on just the same. We continued seeing one another almost nightly. Bars, bars, drinking, drinking! I finally decided to tell the person Jim cared for of his feeling, and to my delight the other person only wanted Jim as a friend. Whenever Jim and I were alone, whether in his apartment, his car, or anywhere alone, we would kiss and kiss like there was no tomorrow! Just kissing him was, to me, sex!

In late September, several of us went to see Shirley Bassey at the Westchester Theater. Great evening!

Still, Jim and I continued seeing each other. Came Halloween, I had another outfit made of silver eyelet, very tight on top, with long sleeves, and a red theater coat to match. Bobby

Garcia did my wig and Jimmy's makeup, as he was going as Count Dracula. We had a fabulous evening. Jim went home for the Thanksgiving holiday. Just before the holiday Bobby Garcia's friend David, who was also a nurse, was hospitalized and operated on for a severe back problem, which would keep him in the hospital until well after Christmas.

Jim returned from his parents' home, and we continued our nightly scene of the bars. He again went home for the Christmas and New Year's holidays.

We had the 1977–78 party at our new apartment. Jim called me at 1:45 A.M. New Year's day to wish me happiness and also to let me know he would be returning January 4, which was a day earlier than anticipated.

By January 6, I had not heard from Jimmy and was disappointed. He wasn't even in the bars. His phone was now disconnected, so I couldn't reach him. I decided to drop him a note. Before I had a chance to mail the letter, he called. All was well, and I asked no questions. We had a big snowstorm on February 6, and my office was closed. Months passed, during which time several of us went to see Mitzi Gaynor at the Westbury Theater. On July 2, Tony Morales and I went once again to P Town. Two weeks later I had a cyst removed from the center of my forehead. How ugly!

After Labor Day, Andy (of Armando and Andy, who had now split up) and I rented a car and we drove to P Town. We found a two-bedroom cottage, and since it was reasonable, took it for the week. We did food shopping and ate in, with Andy doing the cooking. I had several affairs, as did Andy, and before either of us realized it, it was time to return home.

Tony Morales was now seeing someone by the name of Frankie Santos, who lived in Queens. He brought him to our apartment one evening, and we hit it off immediately. True, he was beautiful, but more than that, we got along so very well. I didn't know it at the time, but he and I were to become very close and good friends. Although the affair between Frankie and Tony didn't last, they remained friends, and it was through this association that Tony himself decided to move to Queens, across the street from where Frankie lived.

On Halloween I went as a hooker in a black leotard, black mesh hose, black fringe skirt, and black heels. I had a long, blonde wig that I just frizzed up, and it looked very good. Tom Skouras and my beautiful Jimmy escorted me. We had a ball.

A few weeks after he moved, Tony Morales called and invited Bobby Garcia and me for dinner. Neither of us knew Queens and promptly got lost, especially when I realized we were in New Hyde Park and were on our way to Elmhurst near the shopping center. We called Tony and got directions. We had a very nice time and then hit the local bars.

Several weeks later Tony called to tell me that there was an apartment vacant in his building. I went out and looked at two and decided on one. The evening before I moved, Jimmy and I were in the bars and later he came to my house, and for the first time we made love. It was beautiful, as I knew it would be.

On December 18, I moved in, and that evening with the help of Andy, Bobby, Frankie, and several other friends, had the apartment pretty much in shape. Naturally, I had nothing in the house to eat, and it was late so I couldn't go shopping, and we all were beginning to get a bit hungry. Frankie called his roommate, Jim, and asked him to fix us something, which he did and brought it over. After all, Frankie lived just across the street. Later we went to a bar in Forest Hills, and there were six of us. The bartender asked what we wanted to drink, and one by one we said, "Vodka and grapefruit juice," to which the bartender replied, "Oh, the Citrus Queens have arrived!" To this day, those of us who still drink vodka and grapefruit juice are still known as that. We had a few drinks, and then went to a bar in Jamaica that I had heard of. We liked it and started going on a regular basis.

New Year's Eve of 1978–79 was spent at the bar with Bobby Garcia in full drag, looking very good. His mother, Tony Morales, and myself were also having a good time. Bobby had placed a set of Christmas lights in his wig and every so often would go to an electrical outlet and plug himself in, and the hair would light up; a very amusing sight! He would just stand there and smile.

Andy, who had helped me move, began staying almost nightly at my apartment, so much so that I gave him a set of keys. It annoyed me that he would bring so many people home and sleep on the couch without asking my permission. We were friends, true, but, hey, let's have some consideration! It was months before I had the nerve to tell him I wanted to be alone.

Frankie and I started hanging out together and went everywhere. He introduced me to a Spanish bar called the Bonheur in Elmhurst, and I got to meet many of his friends, including the doorman and the main entertainer. When they saw how well I danced to Latin music, many guys came over and asked me to dance. Nothing sexual (maybe once or twice); just to dance. One night I was there without Frankie, and the owner said he would like to play something for me in English. He played "I Will Survive," which I liked when it first came out, but after hearing it played so often was at a point where I hated it. I thanked him but didn't say a word. I didn't want to hurt his feelings. Whenever he could, the doorman also danced with me, and he was a terrific dancer.

Frankie had now become a full-time bartender and was working on weekends. In February, I had borrowed Tony's car (we were now living in the same building) and went to the bar in Jamaica, where Frankie was now working. While waiting for him to close the bar, I decided to warm up the car. The heavy snow from the night before had now turned to ice, and as I climbed over the embankment, I slipped and fell. Luckily nothing happened!

On March 9, Frankie and I went dancing at an after-hours bar. The next day when I woke up, I was in severe pain. I could hardly walk and had to drag myself across the bedroom floor to the bathroom. After trips back and forth to the doctor, I was diagnosed as having a slipped disc and hospitalized, put in traction, and was in the hospital from April 6 to 12. I had changed medical coverage from Blue Cross to HIP and told my new doctor to also check for diabetes. He informed me that I did not have it. Taking the medication that the other doctor had prescribed for such a long time without having the disease could have killed me, but, of course, I had no way of knowing. My former doctor was so money hungry, and knowing that my medical coverage was very good from my office, he even put in for x-rays that were never taken. I returned to work on May 15, still in occasional pain.

Jimmy DeVito came for a visit and after the rounds of the bars, stayed over. We had carried on once before I moved to Queens, and this was our second time. We were both a bit high, so not much happened other than our embracing, much to my regret!

Frankie was working on my birthday and called to ask me to come up. I had nothing planned, so I went, and the bar was literally empty. During the course of the evening more people arrived, and it turned out to be a nice evening after all. At closing I waited for Frankie, and we took a cab home. Many people in the bars thought that Frankie and I were seeing each other, but, of course, this was not the case.

I met a Colombian man by the name of Luiz at the Spanish bar in August, and we carried on for about a month. Much sex and high phone bills (to Colombia), which he promised to pay but never did.

At an after-hours bar in Jackson Heights in September, I met Allan Luca and went to his place, which was about a block from where I lived. We would become very close friends, but it would take almost a year before that happened.

On Halloween I was invited to a "house party" and wore my Lady in Red outfit (which had not been seen in Queens, you must remember). My escort was a friend who was a bartender and went by the name of Henry, and he wore a striped suit. We looked like a high-priced call girl and her pimp. When we arrived, we went to the basement, where the drinks were being served and after getting our drinks, sat down, and I crossed my legs. As I did, my skirt fell to the left, exposing my legs. Two guys in drag sitting across from us took one look, got up, and left the room. Henry and I looked at each other and smiled, for we both knew I looked good. Later on we were standing near the dancing area, when someone announced over the microphone that the first prize of the evening goes to the Lady in Red. I didn't even know there was a contest and was delighted; not so much for the prize, but the thought alone was a winning factor.

TWENTY-TWO

New Year's Eve of 1979–80 was spent at Tony's apartment. It was larger than mine, but we only had a small group, and it was very nice. I was a new face in Queens, albeit an older one, but nevertheless new and was meeting people very easily. I had a series of one-night stands, what with the bars and the after-hours, I would be home usually about 6:30 A.M.

I was beginning to get slight pains in my chest and thought it best to cut down on smoking, so on January 25 I stopped completely. I haven't had a cigarette since and, believe me, I don't miss it at all!

In May, Frankie and I flew to P Town for the bartenders' awards. We stayed at the Provincetown Inn, which was at the end of town. It was about a ten-minute walk into the town proper. I met a very nice guy and spent the evening with him. We left two days later for Boston to change buses. Since we had a few hours to kill, we went to a bar, where I met someone, as did Frankie. When it came time to leave, neither of us wanted to, and the guy Frankie was with offered his apartment for the night. The guy I was with didn't have a place, and I certainly couldn't invite him to this stranger's house, so we just exchanged addresses. I called my office and told them I wouldn't be in and went to dinner with Frankie and his friend.

The couch was uncomfortable and I had trouble that night sleeping. Frankie, of course, was snug in the bedroom with his friend . The next day, we flew back to New York, but I was so exhausted I called work again and told them I wouldn't be in. All in all, it was some weekend!

In June Steve Cummings and I saw *Sugar Babies* for our birthday, and Bill Bushe gave me a surprise birthday party for my fiftieth with just a few close friends. I couldn't believe it, here I was fifty, and fortunately didn't look, act, or even feel it, for that matter, but time was going by so fast.

Tony and I went to the Cape in September. Nothing very unusual, a few tricks here and there, but we had a good time.

The week before Halloween, one of the after-hours bars had a drag so I took my silver eyelet gown and cut the top to an off-the-shoulder style, and it looked better than the original. I had been in touch with Allan Luca for some time now, and with his new lover, Anthony, along with Tony, I went. We had a ball taking pictures and, in general, just enjoying ourselves.

Andy had moved into my building and had a party on Halloween, which gave me a chance to wear two more outfits (again, not seen in Queens). Oh, the life of a drag!

Once again New Year's Eve of 1980–81 was spent at Tony's. We had a nice crowd, but there was nothing out of the ordinary.

In January, Luiz (the Colombian who owed me money for the phone calls) asked me if he could move in for several weeks. Against my better judgment, I agreed. We didn't have sex, and he still owed money for the phone.

In April I met an attractive Cuban at the Spanish bar by the name of Phil, took him home, and before I knew what happened, he moved in. (When would I learn to stop all this foolishness and get serious about someone?) He wasn't working, and through the efforts of a friend of mine who worked for the unemployment board, he secured a position. Before his first paycheck arrived, he needed to have new glasses. Since he didn't have the money, I paid for them, and to compensate me for it he gave me his frost-free refrigerator, which he had in storage with his furniture in New Jersey. I thought it was a good deal. The refrigerator cost more than the glasses, so I considered the debt paid.

During his stay with me, Ken from California came to New York on a visit and came over to see me one evening. We went to the bars, and later Ken stayed over, sleeping on the sofa. The next morning when I awoke, Phil wasn't in bed, and I assumed he was getting ready for work. I walked into the living room in time to see Phil, completely dressed, walk away from the couch where Ken was sleeping (although at this point he wasn't) and look out the window. I didn't need a rocket scientist to tell me what had transpired but said nothing! Phil went to work, and later Ken left and returned to California the next day.

Andy asked me to take out car insurance for him since he couldn't. His wife, who was also gay, had run her limit, so he was stuck and needed a car. Like a jerk I did, and he eventually ran up parking violations to the tune of three thousand dollars, which took me two years to pay off. Prior to that I had used my credit card to purchase clothes for his son and daughter for school the previous September, and he never paid for that, either. If we were sleeping together, it might have been a different story, but we were just friends at the time. Needless to say, we are no longer friends.

In May I gave a party for Tony Morales's birthday in my apartment with about twenty people, which turned out to be very nice. In June, Jorge from San Juan vacationed here and stayed with me for a few days and was with me for my birthday, when Steve and I saw *42nd Street*. We loved it!

I had to work overtime to help pay Andy's car bill two hours a night, four days a week, then would go to the bar by cab, which my company paid for. During this period, Phil moved, and a bar acquaintance friend of mine moved in. He was a handsome Puerto Rican flight attendant and was hardly ever home. There was no sex involved between us, and we got along beautifully.

Such a convenience! His name was Bobby Milos. He worked on charter flights and would be gone three to four weeks at a time. I told him one time I felt guilty taking his money because he was never home, but he told me not to worry because, after all, his clothes were in my apartment, and he had to spend money to store them someplace.

Once again Tony, Allan, his lover, Anthony, and I went to the Cape in September and had a great time.

For Halloween Bobby Garcia and I, in drag, went to an after-hours bar. I wore my black halter V-neck evening gown, on the top of which, by this time, I had placed pink sequins, and my short, blond wig. Bobby, in my full, black evening skirt, long-sleeved white blouse, and sheer rhinestone theater coat, looked very much the lady!

There was a new disease going around that was killing gay people, and we don't know what caused it. We would learn about this much later.

New Year's Eve of 1981–82 was again spent at Tony's apartment with the usual crowd. Again it turned out very well.

In May, my nephew made his communion, and my sister had a party for him afterwards, which Tony and I attended and had a very good time.

In June, for our birthdays, Steve and I saw *Dreamgirls,* which we thoroughly enjoyed. In August, my niece (my sister Pat's daughter) got married, and we had just the immediate families and had a party for her in Long Island, which Tony, my mom, and I attended.

For Halloween, I borrowed a light green evening gown from Bobby Garcia's mother, which was very tight, especially across the bosom, so much so that I didn't have to wear a bra but just had to stuff the bosom. Bobby wore a pale pink short dress that also belonged to his mother, and with Tom Skouras as my escort and Allan and Anthony, I went to a party in Flushing, stayed for awhile and then hit the after-hours bar.

On New Year's Eve 1982–83 Tony again had his party. It was a big success, and I think everyone had a good time.

Tony gave me a surprise dinner for my birthday with a few friends, including Stan from Long Island, whom I hadn't seen in many years. Bobby Garcia gave me a beautiful plant and told me to take care of it; me, who has no luck with plants! I look at them and they die.

In June Steve and I saw *Evita,* and in November I took my mom to see *Cats,* which was a gift from my coworkers for my twentieth anniversary. My, time does fly!

Again came Halloween, and, this time, the shocker, I didn't go in drag. I had grown a moustache and very thin Abraham Lincoln–type beard and didn't feel like shaving, and I had hoped the kick was wearing off. I would later find out that it hadn't.

In November, off again to San Juan with Bobby. It was such a routine at this point, we didn't even take pictures. Nothing of importance to tell, just a nice vacation.

For New Year's Eve 1983–84, I surprised everyone and had the party at my place. We had a nice crowd, and I enjoyed it very much. *Must do this more often,* I thought, not realizing that it would soon become a ritual for me.

I was going to another Spanish bar in Elmhurst that I liked very much and in May received the Best Customer Award, to which Willy Martinez remarked, "You mean, best lush, don't you?"

I said, "Sweetie, there must have been a close tie because you're right there with me." He smiled and agreed.

In June we saw *La Cage aux Folles,* and it was back to the Cape in September with Tony and Allan and a nut Tony was seeing at the time, whose name I can't remember.

Halloween came, and this year I had a friend make me an electric blue, off-the-shoulder, long-sleeved tight evening gown. I wore a new blonde-on-blonde wig, which Bobby Garcia fixed for me. The outfit was topped off with a white feather boa, which

I recently bought. We went to the local bars and had a wonderful time.

Willy Martinez was seeing an attractive, prematurely grey-haired man by the name of Richard Smith, whom upon meeting I liked immediately. When New Year's Eve 1984–85 rolled around, Richard offered his apartment. It was large and had a terrace. At midnight we all went on the terrace and screamed like teenagers.

On January 2, Steve and I saw *Torch Song Trilogy* and in June saw *The Tap Dance Kid*. When I moved to Queens, Steve and I only saw one another on our birthdays, but now we were doing the scene twice a year, which was great.

In August, Tony, Allan, and I went to the Cape and to San Juan in September.

That year for Halloween, I purchased a Greek-style evening gown, to which I added silver sequins to the hem and borders of the gown. Bobby again did my new strawberry blonde wig in a Grecian style. The white feather boa from last year finished the outfit, and Tom Skouras was my escort.

We again moved the 1985–86 party back to Tony Morales, which, with my new "us" crowd, turned out very well. On February 15, I saw *Jerry's Girls* with Steve.

Allan and I went to San Juan in April and I met another guy named Luiz, and, at my age, stupidly brought him back to New York. I suppose behind it all I was looking for someone special to be with and jumped too fast. I had a birthday party for him in May, and in June Steve and I saw *Sweet Charity*.

In September we hit the Cape again, and November saw us back in San Juan. This time I brought Luiz back with me and left him there. Too much trouble!

Ken in California called to say good-bye. He was dying of AIDS, and I could hardly hear him. He and Bill Lopez had been broken up for many years, but were still living together. Bill got on the phone and told me he had found him on the floor just the day before; he was that weak. I didn't know what to say and told him to hang on because the doctors were coming out with new drugs every day. On December 3, he passed away.

It was all around us, everywhere you looked. Friends and bar acquaintances alike were dying one after the other from this dreaded disease called AIDS, which I briefly spoke about earlier, and it was frightening. They found a medication called AZT that helps, but there is still no complete cure. I pray there will be one soon.

The 1986–87 party was again held at Richard's and at midnight the usual screaming on the terrace, but it was a fun evening. On February 2nd, I saw Yma Sumac with Bobby Milos and on March 3rd saw her again with John Edison, whom I hadn't seen in ages but we did keep in touch by phone.

On March 30, we had a birthday party for Willy Martinez at the Spanish bar. From the pictures we saw later, we must have had one hellva time.

In May it was back to San Juan with Allan and Bobby Garcia. I saw my dear friend Esther, whom I had known from my days with the movie company. She was living there now and looked wonderful. During our conversation Bobby asked her how long she had been living in San Juan. She said, "Seventeen years!" Then he asked how long it had taken her to learn Spanish and she said, "Seventeen years!" We all had a chuckle on that.

Steve and I saw *Me and My Girl* on our birthday, which we both enjoyed.

In August, the Spanish bar had a small birthday get-to-gether downstairs for one of the entertainers who appeared there and who had told me he had AIDS. Such a beautiful-looking boy. What a shame! But this was 1987 and we still had much to learn about it. We were to learn how to protect ourselves, and I for one, the few times I did go with someone, used protection even before we were told officially to do so. I think this is the reason I'm still here and tested negative recently.

The party was for selected customers and I felt very proud that I was asked, especially since I was the only American (other than the owner's lover) who was invited.

This year no drag. Was it really fading?

New Year's Eve 1987–88 would be held at my place for the next seven years. I even wore a bow tie for the occasion. My beard was long gone but the moustache remained.

In June, Steve and I saw *Anything Goes*, which I thoroughly enjoyed because I adore Cole Porter's music. In July, Marie O'Toole passed away of cancer and a coworker had named Glen, whose roommate had done my original red gown, also died of an embolism. Very sad year.

Again no drag for Halloween.

New Year's Eve 1988–89 was at my place. In late January, I met a boy named Mario, and we started seeing each other. In February, another bar acquaintance named Hugo gave us a big party at his apartment, and we had a wonderful time. However, this affair ended about a week later when we went to a Spanish bar and he started flirting with one of the customers. I got pissed off and left. That was the end of us romantically, but we did remain friends.

In April, it was San Juan again with Tony Morales, and in June I gave myself a birthday party. When I saw the pictures and how much weight I had gained, there was no doubt as to why I hadn't been going in drag. I was a balloon! That 122 pounds I had started off with was up to 160, and I didn't like it, so I put myself on a diet. No wonder I wasn't meeting anyone; not that I was actually looking!

Also in June, Steve and I saw *Jerome Robbins' Broadway*. August saw my twenty-fifth anniversary of employment with the firm, and they gave me a very nice party, to which Tony Morales and Willy Martinez came.

One of our favorite bars in Jackson Heights closed on July 13, and another would open on October 10 two blocks away, but I started going to a bar in Forest Hills where Allan Luca was hanging out, and for the next two years that was my "home."

It was there one evening I met Chuck James, who was about ten years my junior. He was very nice, and through him I met his lover, Bob, and their neighbor Paul. Chuck and Bob had been going together since they were in their early twenties. I enjoyed Chuck's company, and we met almost nightly since he also worked nights at the time. Neither of us were interested sexually; we were just friends.

Once again, no drag for Halloween that year.

New Year's Eve 1989–90 I invited Chuck and my new friends and had the party at my place. Between the people I had met in Forest Hills and the people I knew in Jackson Heights, I had quite a turnout, and everyone seemed to get along very well.

In May, Chuck and several of the people from the bar and I went on a gay boat ride up the Hudson River. We had a wonderful time. In June, Steve and I saw *City of Angels*, which we enjoyed.

A friend of mine in Texas, named Robin, who I had met back in 1975 and with whom I had a brief affair but had kept in touch with over the years, passed away from AIDS. Another friend and bartender of many years, by the name of Denny, also died of an undisclosed ailment. I was shocked to learn that Connie Lucia had died of a heart attack only a few months after taking an early retirement at the age of sixty-two. This was turning out to be a very sad year for me.

In September, Allan and I went to the Cape and rented a two-bedroom condo, went food shopping, and set up light housekeeping for the week. There was also a friend of Allan's, by the name of Jim, who took a room in the main house around the corner and came over for dinner each night. Jim and I had flown up from New York while Allan drove, and we were to drive back with him.

For years many people had told me that they had seen Cliff Wayne performing on the Cape. I kept saying no because he was too big a name for a small town like P Town. I told them they must have him confused with another artist. To my surprise and delight, he had called me before I left on vacation to tell me he would be appearing in P Town. "If it wasn't for the money they're paying, you wouldn't see me in a dump like this. I mean, really, Tommy, beer cans in the back, oh, please!" he said to me later that evening at dinner after his performance.

We hadn't seen each other in many years, but the conversation picked up as if we had seen each other every day. It was terrific, and Allan just stared at him in amazement. Here he was, sitting and having dinner at the same table with one of the biggest names in show business. It was a wonderful evening, but it ended all too soon. Cliff had to be up early in the morning for his return to California.

In late September, my sister Pat and I decided to give Mom a surprise party for her eightieth birthday at Pat's home in Connecticut. Tony Morales and I got lost on the way up, and I had to call Pat for further directions. Mom was under the impression that she was merely going for dinner, but when my sister Mary and her family arrived from New Jersey, she figured something was up.

"It's a surprise party for you, Mom," I said, and we all clapped and kissed her, took movies, and pictures. She was so surprised and pleased and I saw tears fill her eyes. The afternoon went along very well, and in the early evening we all left for the drive back to New York and New Jersey.

New Year's Eve 1990–91, I decided to go in drag. The feeling was back, even if I was now over sixty. I guess it had never gone away. Who cared? I had lost enough weight and decided to purchase a dress. I ordered a street-length dress consisting of gold metallic material that looked like a pullover blouse that tied in a bow below the hips. Under that was a light black dress with a full skirt that gave the impression that the skirt was pleated. A short, dirty blond wig and gold sandals completed the outfit. The people I had invited were again from both Jackson Heights and Forest Hills, so I had a house full and loved it. We made a video tape, which turned out to be rather amusing.

When the party ended we went to the Forest Hills bar, which was jammed, but I had no trouble getting a seat. I knew most of the people, and one guy got up and graciously gave me his seat. We took pictures and had a wonderful time.

We went on another gay boat ride on a beautiful sunny day in May, after which we went to one of the midtown bars for cocktail hour. When we arrived we were the only people there because it was four o'clock, and the bar had just opened. There were seven of us at that point. We had a few drinks, and then Chuck drove me back to Queens, and the others took their cars to Long Island.

In June, Steve and I saw *Grand Hotel,* which we also thoroughly enjoyed. In July, Allan and I once again went to the Cape and took the same condo we had had the year before. Allan's friend Jim took the same room in the building around the corner. On Sunday, Allan woke me and said that we had to take Jim to the hospital. He had AIDS, and we knew it, but while last year he was fine, this year he had lost so much weight and couldn't control his bowel movements. It was a very rainy day as we drove to Hyannis and to the emergency room.

The doctors took him, and he was gone, so Allan and I went to the cafeteria to get something to eat. It was closed, and all they had were machines. We both had money, but the only change we had was enough for one cup of coffee and one hamburger, which we shared. We returned to find out how Jim was doing and were told it would be at least another hour. We decided that since it was chilly we would take the car and go shopping for something heavy to wear and get something decent to eat, which we did. When we returned, they told us Jim had been discharged. We looked everywhere, but he couldn't be found. We even had him paged and still no answer! Allan went into the emergency room and looked around and found him in the bathroom, trying to put his pants back on. We finally got him to the car and put him in the back seat, where he slept, and returned to P Town. It was noon when we had arrived in Hyannis, and it was now 7:00 P.M. We arrived at 8:00 P.M., and Jim went to his room and made arrangements with the management to fly back to New York the following afternoon.

Allan drove him to the airport, and when the plane was ready, I helped him up, and we watched as he boarded. I said to Allan, "You know, I don't think he'll make it to Christmas."

"I know!" replied Allan.

Shortly after our return, I went to the Forest Hills bar one Friday night, and Chuck James was there. We were talking when the DJ, whom I didn't like to begin with, started in on me about my complaint regarding some of the songs he played. I was handling the situation very well when the manager, who was a friend of his, came to his defense. Chuck and the manager went into the street and talked while I continued my argument with the DJ.

The manager and Chuck had come in from the street and were standing next to me as I ordered another drink. The manager told the bartender to make it weak, to which I replied, "Listen, you're going to charge me four dollars for a weak drink? I could go to a certain bar in Manhattan, and for the same price get a drink that will knock your socks off. I don't need this! I don't have to come here and put up with this. There are too many other bars that will be happy to take my money. I'll just go someplace else!"

To which he replied, "Please do!"

So ended my Forest Hills association, and I returned to the bar in Jackson Heights that had opened two years before. I had heard rumors that I had been kicked out of the bar, and every time I heard this would set the people straight. I had *not* been thrown out; I left of my own free will and was happy about it.

A few days before Thanksgiving, Allan called me and told me that Jim had passed away. When I look back, that was a very sad vacation that week for both of us.

I didn't bother with drag for Halloween, and for New Year's Eve 1991–92 the party again was at my place with our usual "us" crowd, which, of course, makes for an enjoyable evening.

The AIDS virus was now spreading to the straight community, especially drug users who used needles. It seems the virus is contained in the blood. Since I had never done drugs, I had no problem.

That year would start off bad and will always remain a sad year in my heart. My dear friend Tom Skouris died in January of complications that started off with a toothache that turned cancerous, and the radiation treatments he was taking killed him. In February, another friend, named Memo, who was a bartender in the Elmhurst Spanish bar, also passed away from AIDS.

My mother, who had been in and out of hospitals for about two years, was once again in the hospital with a slight heart condition. That's what the hospital told us. On March 31, my brother called to tell me that she had died the day before, but no one had informed either him or me. Besides being very upset at the thought of losing her, I was furious with the hospital for not informing us for over twenty-six hours after she had died. I called and complained, but I might as well have been talking to the wall for all the satisfaction I got.

Mom was eighty-two and a half and had had a good life. I made arrangements with a friend who is a funeral director. He came over to my house, and we did all the paper work. She had died on Monday, it was now late Tuesday evening, and she wouldn't be ready for viewing until Thursday. I left a note in Tony's mailbox giving all the information and told him he'd better come to the wake on Thursday because Mom had treated him like a third son.

When I arrived at the funeral home on Thursday and saw her, I had to hold back the tears. I figured if I showed emotion the rest of my family would follow, so I tried to be brave for them. I noticed that the coffin was not the one I had selected, and when my friend the funeral director arrived, I asked him about it.

"When I saw the clothes that your sisters decided on and put your mom in she didn't look right, I selected the silver casket because it went very well with the pink and black suit she was wearing."

I thanked him and told him she looked wonderful. He had upgraded the coffin and didn't charge me, for which I was also very thankful. A priest came in, and we said prayers and then some of my friends came. There was Willy Martinez and his roommate Joel (who remarked that I resembled my mother), who had never met my mother, and Richard James, who also, had never met Mom. Millie and George, whom I hadn't seen in many years, came because they knew Mother when she lived in Brooklyn in the house next to them about the time of my sister Pat's accident many years ago. As the time for closing approached, two more friends, Peter and Alex, who also had never met my mother, arrived. Still no sign of Tony, and it upset me. Of all the people I knew, he should have been there.

The morning of the funeral, I took a cab to Mother's apartment in Brooklyn. My brother and his wife had been living there for some time and Pat (my sister-in-law) had been taking care of Mother during her illness. I think of all the family, she took it the worst. She really loved Mom, and I think that's unusual for a daughter-in-law, and it was very sweet.

We went to the funeral home and said our final good-byes to Mom and then across the street to the church for Mass. During the Mass, I looked around and saw Tony standing in the back of the church. Willy Martinez had arrived earlier and was standing next to me. When the Mass was over and the coffin taken to the hearse, I thanked Tony for coming, and since he already knew where she was being buried, he and Willy drove behind us to the Bronx. After the priest said prayers, Willy and Tony left because Tony had to go to work. We returned to my mother's apartment to have something to eat, acknowledge the Mass cards we had received, and distribute several different articles that we all wanted.

My sister Pat drove me home, and during our conversation she said, "You handled everything so beautifully. Mom looked great. And I didn't see you show any emotion."

"Yes, they did a beautiful job on her, and I couldn't show any emotions. If I had, you all would have been wrecks."

"Yes, I guess you're right."

She dropped me off at my apartment, and I went upstairs. Once in the apartment, all the emotion I had built up all week came out, and I cried for what seemed like hours.

There was another gay boat ride in May, and Chuck James and our crowd from Forest Hills all went and had a great time. In June, Steve and I saw *Crazy For You*, and Willy Martinez and I gave a small party for Peter's birthday in September.

My former roommate Terry, who had stayed with me for a short period when I lived on West 107th Street, died of AIDS, as did another fellow coworker who lived in my building, by the name of Bob. Dick Dawson died of a liver ailment. This was some year. As I said earlier, it was one of the saddest I've ever had.

In October, Hugo (who had given me the party when I was seeing Mario) opened a gay bar in Jackson Heights, and our crowd went to the opening. On Halloween I decided to go in drag again and took my black halter with the pink sequins and replaced them with rhinestones. My wig was short, platinum blond, very curly, and some people said that if Marilyn Monroe were alive I would probably look something like her. I was very flattered!

While Mom was alive, I continued to work, in case she needed anything such as an air-conditioner or an easy chair or whatever. After her death, I figured it was about time to retire, so on December 31 I did. I could have retired after twenty years with the firm at age fifty-five, but then I couldn't collect Social Security, so I thought this was a good time. If Mom hadn't died, I would have continued working for at least three more years. I had a private party at one coworker's apartment, and it was very nice. They also had a spread for me the night I left.

Tony Morales and his new lover of a few years, Al, moved to Glen Cove. I felt a bit lonely knowing he wasn't in the building any longer, but time would take care of that, like it always does.

New Year's Eve 1992–93 was spent at my apartment. It was a very nice crowd, but once again nothing out of the ordinary occurred.

My hair was on the long side when Mom died, and I didn't cut it for a year. It was in a ponytail when, at the end of March, my brother, sister-in-law, niece, and her boyfriend drove me to the cemetery for the first anniversary of Mom's passing. My brother also wore his hair the same way. He asked why my hair was lighter than his, and I told him it was because I was older than him and much greyer.

In May my hairdresser died of AIDS; in June another friend named Frank. Steve and I saw *Kiss of the Spider Woman,* which was now a musical, and enjoyed it.

In September, Jaime, the manager of the Spanish bar in Elmhurst and also the exlover of Memo, died of AIDS in South America. Andy (he of the car bit years back) also died of AIDS, which didn't surprise me as much as many others. These are just people I associated with, not to mention the countless number of bar acquaintances whose names never appear in this book. I now go to the bars only to socialize; nothing else. I hadn't been with anyone in years because of the AIDS bit.

On Halloween I decided to go in drag one more time. I wore the gold and black outfit I had worn at my New Year's Eve party in 1990, only this time I wore the platinum blond wig from last year. Chuck James was my escort, and we just went to a local bar. Nice evening but no great shakes.

New Year's Eve 1993–94: best party in a long time. Steve sent me a card saying he didn't want to go out on our birthdays anymore. He said he was in a midlife crisis; hells bells, that's nothing more than male menopause. We all go through it; I did!

In early March, my new hairdresser, an attractive Puerto Rican (what else?) by the name of Jose, whom I had known for many years, cut my hair very short. I wear it combed forward in the Caesar look. It is also natural, being very blond in the front and silvery grey on the remaining part of the head. It's comfortable, and I like it. Very easy to keep.

Everyone was shocked when we found out that Hugo, who had just opened a bar about a year and half ago had died of AIDS-related complications. He had been in a coma for two weeks prior to his passing. We were also shocked to learn of the motorcycle accident death of little Joey, who was the ex-lover of one of my favorite bartenders. Just the week before Joey and I had been talking in the bar, and he said he was going home because he was low on money. I asked him to stay and chat with me and brought him a drink. I suppose between the booze and drugs, his death came instantly—at least he didn't suffer!

I had been going nightly to one bar in Jackson Heights that I liked very much. The morning of August 30 would be a date that I will never forget. I arrived, as usual, about midnight and was seated at the bar next to a very young, good-looking Italian boy (haven't we heard this somewhere before?). I was in conversation with the bartender, and then the young boy and I struck up a conversation. Strictly general. We talked for some time, and he seemed very pleasant and nice to talk with, so when he was leaving I gave him my phone number. I figured perhaps I could have another nice friend. To my delight, he called two days later and came over.

His name was Alex Monroe, and he was old enough to be my (get this) grandson. We didn't do anything sexually, and for the days that followed, he would just call me, and at times we would meet at the bar.

I was beginning to feel something that I hadn't felt in years for this man, and I knew it was wrong but didn't care. Then it happened! We started kissing and making love, but in a safe way, and I knew I was falling in love with him. They say, "There's no fool like an old fool," and perhaps they are right.

New Year's Eve 1994–95 was here, with the usual party at my apartment, which turned out very well. Alex arrived late because he had to work that day. We had a great time, and it felt wonderful to be with someone special on New Year's Eve.

I took Alex to dinner for his birthday in January to a very nice bar in the Village called Five Oaks, which he loved. We also went to hear a woman with whom I used to work sing, and he loved this as well. He wasn't working when we met, but he is now, and it's difficult for us to see each other.

I don't recall ever receiving a Valentine's Day card, but I was shocked to receive one from Bill Lopez, of all people—forty-five years later. As I said before, he's one fun person!

Also on Valentine's Day of 1995, I bought Alex a little teddy bear that he thought was the cutest. I liked it myself and wanted to buy one, but the one I had bought was the last one they had. I made pot roast for dinner, and when he wasn't looking slipped a ring in the champagne glass. When he saw it, his eyes lit up in amazement. "It's beautiful!" he said. "I love you so much."

What more can an old man ask for? He's young, he's beautiful, and I trust and believe in him. No more cruising! Yes, I still go to the bars to socialize, but nothing more. We talk daily, and he comes over on his days off. I think after all these years I've finally met the one for me. A bit late, perhaps, but better late than not at all. We've been together eight months already, and this is the longest I've been with anyone in my life, as you have just witnessed. I'm the happiest I've been in years. Wish me luck, dear readers. Who said gay stories don't have happy endings? This one does!

EPILOGUE

So, dear reader, you have just completed almost forty-five years in the life of a semi–drag queen. I've had fun and would do it all over the exact same way if I had the opportunity. I'm sorry to have lost so many wonderful friends, but such is life!

I can't believe that when I started this book, I was only nineteen years old. I turn sixty-five in June of 1995. As I said earlier, where did the time go? Someone said a long time ago that "Youth is wasted on the young." How very true! I've seen how people lied to me, took advantage of me, and still I loved them in my own way because of my youth. I doubt today any of those things would happen. I just wouldn't have let it.

I'm happy to report that many of the people I knew when I was very young are fortunately still with us. I haven't seen Harold or Allen (Terry's cousin) in many years, so I don't know about them. George Jennings, Jerry Leighman, Bill Lopez, Joe Davidson, Helenmae, Al, Eric Johns, Johnny Tyler, Bob Kent, Phil Conway, Stan Gordon (who, incidentally, stopped by my apartment in June of 1994), Chuck Douglas, Bobby Garcia, Bob Lanza, Cliff Wayne, Ray and Harry, Tony Morales, Willy Martinez, Frank Santos, Bobby Milos, Richard Smith, Chuck James, Allan Luca, Jimmy DeVito, Steve Cummings, to name a few, I still keep in touch with from time to time, even if it's just with a Christmas card.

I hope you've enjoyed reliving my life. I know I had a ball writing it, and it brought back such pleasant and unpleasant times. One doesn't get a chance to relive one's life very often, and in doing this book, that's exactly what I did, and the memories it brought made me feel so good inside. Thank you for reading this, and be careful in all your endeavors. Live life to the fullest and enjoy it! Time slips by too quickly!